ype of Cropani's boa, *Corallus cropanii*, from Miracatu, , Brazil. This species is arguably the rarest boa in the t undoubtedly the rarest in the New World. Photograph f Alma R. Hoge.

KALEIDOSCOP

THE GENUS *CORALLUS* (

The I
São I
world
court

Kaleidoscopic Tree Boas

The Genus *Corallus* of Tropical America

Peter J. Stafford & Robert W. Henderson

KRIEGER PUBLISHING COMPANY
MALABAR, FLORIDA
1996

Cover: A captive-bred neonate Emerald tree boa at 23 days old.
Photograph: Peter J. Stafford.

Original Edition 1996

Printed and Published by
KRIEGER PUBLISHING COMPANY
KRIEGER DRIVE
MALABAR, FLORIDA 32950

Copyright © 1996 by Krieger Publishing Company

Library of Congress Cataloging-In-Publication Data

Stafford, Peter J.
    Kaleidoscopic tree boas : the genus *Corallus* of tropical America /
Peter J. Stafford and Robert W. Henderson.
        p.   cm.
    Includes bibliographical references (p.   ) and index.
    ISBN 0-89464-975-2 (hardcover : alk. paper)
    1. Tree boas—Latin America. 2. Captive snakes. I. Henderson,
Robert W., 1945–   . II. Title.
    QL666.063S725   1996
    597.96—dc20   95-49034
                                                             CIP

10 9 8 7 6 5 4 3 2

PETER J. STAFFORD

To my parents

ROBERT W. HENDERSON

To my son,
KY HENDERSON,
in fond remembrance
of tree boa hunting in Grenada,
and mosquito bites, playing catch, KFC,
stinging ants, *Acacia* thorns, Grand Anse Beach,
sheep on the fairway, and the road block

CONTENTS

THE AUTHORS

Peter J. Stafford works as a research scientist and curator in the Department of Botany at The Natural History Museum, London. A keen naturalist, he has pursued an active interest in reptiles and amphibians since early childhood and has published regularly on the subject of herpetology, including papers on natural history and captive husbandry, and three books on snakes and lizards. Recently he has developed a special interest in the herpetology of Central America and other parts of the New World tropics. Following a number of expeditions and field studies on the herpetofauna of Belize, he is presently working on a comprehensive account of the reptiles of this country.

Robert W. Henderson is curator of herpetology at the Milwaukee Public Museum. He is author of more than 120 technical articles on amphibian and/or reptile biology and has coauthored or edited five other books on reptiles. Although he is primarily interested in snakes, his research has included field work on amphibians and other reptiles as well. For the past 15 years he has concentrated on the West Indian fauna, visiting more than 40 islands in his search for snakes. More recently, he has focused on neotropical boas (in the West Indies and on the neotropical mainland) with a strong emphasis on diet and foraging behavior. Enamoured with tree boas as a boy, he has been studying their biology for 8 years. His work with *Corallus*, as well as other boas, is ongoing.

ACKNOWLEDGMENTS

For help received while preparing this book we extend grateful thanks to Nancy Garwood, who assisted in producing the maps; Colin McCarthy and the Lower Vertebrates Division of The Natural History Museum, London; Okan Güney for allowing his animals and captive breeding setup to be photographed; David Blody and the Fort Worth Zoo; Marian J. Short, Lynne Speake, Steven Simpson, and the following for use of their photographs: Hans E.A. Boos, Rose M. Henderson, Alma R. Hoge, William F. Holmstrom, Kirsten Kranz, William W. Lamar, Mark O'Shea, Giuseppe Puorto, Richard S. Reed, W. Carl Taylor, and R. Allan Winstel.

Henderson's field work with boids in general and tree boas in particular has been generously funded by the Milwaukee Public Museum, the Central Florida Herpetological Society, Jack A. Puelicher, the late Albert Schwartz, the Wildlife Conservation Society, Robert W. Bourgeois, Sr., and the Robert W. Bourgeois, Jr. family. He has been accompanied in the field by Hans E.A. Boos, Jacques Daudin, Joel Friesch, Gary T. Haas, Ky F. Henderson, Rose M. Henderson, James and Kirsten Kranz, Timothy J. McCarthy, Richard A. Sajdak, and R. Allan Winstel. Henderson is appreciative of the cooperation he has received from the

Forestry Division on St. Vincent and the Grenadines (Brian Johnson, Calvin Nicholls, and Cornelius Richards), and the Ministry of Agriculture's Forestry Division (Alan Joseph and Rolax Frederick) and the Department of National Parks (George Vincent) on Grenada. On Trinidad, Hans Boos arranged exciting excursions, and Howard Nelson of the Wildlife Section (Forestry Division) arranged for his permits. In Venezuela, tree boa hunting, fun to begin with, was made even more pleasurable by the company of Courtney Anderson, Tibisay Escalona, Bill Holmstrom, María Muñoz, Tony Ratten, Jesús Rivas, and John Thorbjarnarson. Lastly, Henderson is grateful to the personnel associated with collections who so generously loaned him many hundreds of specimens of *Corallus*; they will be more thoroughly acknowledged in a future publication.

INTRODUCTION

As dusk turned to night on the West Indian island of Grenada, a biologist stopped his jeep at the side of a narrow dirt road and prepared himself for an evening's work. Dressed in jeans, a long-sleeved shirt, and stout leather boots, he fitted a battery to his belt. Attached to the battery was a slender cord leading to a light fastened by an elastic band around his head. He took a few seconds to focus the light so that the beam was as concentrated as possible, and then slung a small bag over his shoulder containing some cloth and plastic bags, thermometers, scales and rules for weighing and measuring animals, insect repellant, and a couple of granola bars for sustenance. In addition, he carried a clipboard with pre-printed sheets of paper listing the range of habitat variables he wanted to record. Picking up a long slender bamboo pole that he had left at the site the night before, he headed down the track through darkened stands of banana, sugar cane, cacao, citrus, mango and breadfruit trees, confident that he would certainly not see another vehicle and most likely no other people. The night around him resounded to the chirping of insects, dogs barking on distant hills, and the amorous, high-pitched call of *Eleutherodactylus*

1

johnstonei, a species of frog now almost ubiquitous on islands in the Lesser Antilles.

Almost immediately his headlamp caught the eye-shine of an animal about 10 meters up in a tree, but when he could see that its two eyes were facing him, he quickly realized he was looking at a Common opossum (*Didelphis marsupialis*), and not the quarry he was searching for. Several minutes later, however, sweeping the beam of his headlamp over the walls of vegetation on either side of him, the light detected a solitary red-orange glow, slowly moving near the end of a branch on a mango tree about 3 meters above the ground. The telltale eye-shine was caused by the light from the headlamp being reflected back by a mirroring device in the animal's eye called the *tapetum lucidum*. The biologist knew he had found what he was looking for: a snake belonging to the tree boa genus *Corallus*.

The snake that was crawling slowly and purposefully along a nearly horizontal branch of the mango tree had earlier spent the day coiled in a tight ball, possibly in the same tree in which it was now foraging. It was dull yellow in color with only a faint hint of a dorsal pattern. Its head looked large and bulbous compared to its slender neck, and its body was elongated and laterally compressed. The herpetologist removed a pencil from his breast pocket and began taking notes. He recorded information about the tree, the particular branch of the tree, the foliage, the proximity of other trees and bushes, time of night, moon phase, activity of the snake, and more. Once he was sure he had jotted down all the desired data, he set his bag and clipboard on the ground and raised the bamboo pole to the branch on which the tree boa was crawling. Maneuvering the pole under the middle part of the snake's body, he gently exerted lifting force to dislodge it. The strongly prehensile tail began to loosen its hold and the snake was freed from its arboreal anchor. Quickly the herpetologist lowered the pole and prepared to grab the defensively aggressive snake. It made a sudden lunging strike, catching him unaware and snagging a finger with its long anterior-most teeth, though quickly withdrew. The herpetologist smiled to himself and gave silent approval to the snake's wonderfully irascible behavior; it was one of many reasons he liked tree boas. Another attempt was made to grasp the tree boa behind its head, this time successfully, and the animal was put into a cloth bag. As he jotted down some additional notes, the biologist inadvertently looked up into an adjacent mango tree and the beam from his headlamp detected another glowing eye-shine; he knew it was going to be a good night. For the next 4 hours he would continue his search for tree boas and record a variety of data, releasing the snakes shortly after capturing them. Slowly, over days and weeks in the field, a picture of how tree boas make their living would begin to emerge.

* * *

The tree boas (genus *Corallus*) of tropical America are regarded as a highly specialized group adapted for life in the trees. Among herpetoculturists they have a deserved reputation for being rather bad-tempered but, despite this, their striking appearance and often exorbitant coloration have long made them popular exhibits for zoological display. At times they can indeed be difficult to handle, and they never really lose their inclination to bite, but it seems clear there will always be a devout band of enthusiasts interested in keeping these unusual members of the boa family.

Four species are currently recognized in the genus *Corallus*: the Common tree boa (*Corallus hortulanus*[1]), with two subspecies; the Emerald tree boa (*C. caninus*); the Annulated tree boa (*C. annulatus*), with three subspecies; and Cropani's boa (*C. cropanii*), a species known until fairly recently by the name of *Xenoboa cropanii*. Tree boas were first described by Linnaeus in 1758, and since then they have appeared under a host of different species names; a specimen of *C. hortulanus* was once even given the name *"Vipera bitis"*, presumably through the resem-

---

[1]It has been recently determined by McDiarmid et al. (in press) that the correct name for the species long referred to as *Corallus enydris* (Linnaeus) is actually *Corallus hortulanus* (Linnaeus).

blance of its large head and front teeth to those of vipers. The presently accepted generic name, *Corallus*, is derived from the Latin word "coral", a possible reference to the dorsal coloration in some juveniles of *C. hortulanus*. It was first used in the description of *Corallus obtusirostris* in 1803 (now placed in synonymy with *C. hortulanus*), and was resurrected in 1951 by Forcart.

We have prepared this book in order to summarize what is currently known about the natural history of New World tree boas and, with the increasing popularity of herpetoculture in general, and boid snakes in particular, we felt a melding of natural history and husbandry was pertinent. Herpetoculturists will be better and more responsibly prepared to maintain a particular species in captivity if they are aware of the animal's requirements in the wild; likewise, observations made of animals in captivity under proper conditions can often complement those made of the same species in the field.

TREE BOAS AND THEIR RELATIVES

When the snake is in motion . . . , if he can be induced to move in sunlight he presents a remarkably beautiful appearance. The dull dark brown seems to change to a rich mosaic, over which shimmers a lovely bluish iridescence as he wends his sinuous way along the branches.

—Mole and Urich (1894), describing *Corallus hortulanus* on Trinidad

The genus *Corallus* belongs to the family Boidae, which may or may not include the pythons (depending on whose classification you disagree with least). More importantly, tree boas are members of the subfamily Boinae which includes, among others, the famous *Boa constrictor* and the Common anaconda (*Eunectes murinus*), arguably the longest snake species in the world, but undoubtedly the most massive. The subfamily has an enigmatic and controversial distribution; although most species occur in the Neotropics, additional species also occur on Madagascar and Réunion (*Acrantophis* and *Sanzinia*; Kluge [1991] synonymized these two genera with *Boa*, and subsequent mitochondrial DNA sequencing data have supported the close affinities of *Boa* and *Acrantophis* [Forstner et al., 1995]) and in the Indoaustralian Ar-

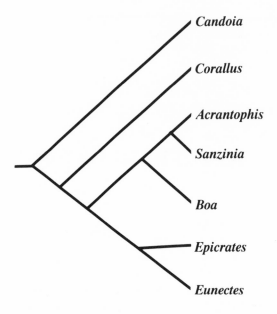

Candoia

Corallus

Acrantophis

Sanzinia

Boa

Epicrates

Eunectes

Figure 1.   Relationships among boine genera. Modified from Kluge (1991).

chipelago (*Candoia*), but our discussion will focus on the New World representatives of the subfamily (Figure 1). Boine relatives of tree boas are illustrated in Plates 1–5.

Ten species of boines occur on the neotropical mainland, representing four genera (1 species of *Boa*, 4 species of *Corallus*, 1 species of *Epicrates*, 4 species of *Eunectes*). The West Indies (Bahamas, Greater Antilles, Virgin Islands) harbor nine species of *Epicrates* endemic to the region (Tolson and Henderson, 1993), plus *Boa* and *Corallus* occur at the southern end of the Lesser Antilles, with *Boa* occurring as far north as Dominica. Kluge (1991) concluded that "boines have had a long and continuous presence in the New World, at least since the divergence of *Corallus* and (*Boa* (*Epicrates*, *Eunectes*)) . . . ." *Boa constrictor* (Plate 1) has the widest range of the New World boines and one of the widest distributions of any snake species in the world (ca. 66° of latitude, from northern Mexico south into Argentina), including a wide insular distribution (Henderson et al., 1995). It is a primarily ground-dwelling species that attains a maximum snout-vent length (SVL) of about 4.5 m. It occurs in a wide variety of habitats (from rain forests to deserts), and it has a very catholic diet, preying on fishes, lizards, birds, and a wide range (taxonomically and size) of mammals. The lone mainland representative of the genus *Epicrates* is *E. cenchria* (Plate 2). It too has a broad geographic range (ca. 38° of latitude), occurs in a wide variety of habitats, is largely ground-dwelling, and exploits lizards, birds, and mammals as food (Henderson et al., 1995); it attains a maximum SVL of about 2.0 m. The anacondas (*Eunectes*) are largely aquatic. The most familiar species, *E. murinus* (Plates 3 and 4), has a geographic range that covers about 35° of latitude in habitats that include rain forest and llanos. Its maximum length is a popular and controversial topic, but a conservative estimate would put it at about 8.0 m; less conservative guesses put it in excess of 10.0 m. The Common anaconda preys on a wide taxonomic and size range of vertebrate prey, including fishes, lizards, snakes, crocodilians, birds (including storks), and mammals (including Capybara and White-tail deer) (Henderson et al., 1995).

In contrast to the more massive boa constrictor and anacondas, the tree boas are, morphologically, a rather delicate group of snakes. Of necessity for their arboreal existence, they must be. It seems likely that proto-*Corallus* took to the trees in order to exploit previously unexploited resources, trees and tree-dwelling prey, and to avoid potential competition from its relatives. Two species of *Corallus* (*caninus* and *hortulanus*) are widely sympatric with three other boines (*Boa constrictor*, *Epicrates cenchria*, and *Eunectes murinus*), all of which are more massive and ground-dwelling. *Epicrates cenchria* is the closest to *Corallus* in terms of body proportions, whereas *B. constrictor* and *E. murinus* attain much greater length and weight. The anacondas take prey that is predominantly associated with aquatic habitats in South America, and the boa constrictor is a generalist that will opportunistically take a wonderfully wide range of prey associated with many kinds of habitats. Since snakes are gape-limited, large size allows a snake to exploit a wider range of prey types and sizes, and smaller boines, such as the tree boas, are restricted to smaller prey. By taking to the trees, boines could spatially and trophically exploit resources unavailable to the more massive ground-dwelling species. Among the neotropical boines, species of *Corallus* have evolved the most specialized body shape, including a laterally compressed body, a slender neck with a large head, a strongly prehensile tail, well-developed heat-sensitive labial pits capable of detecting temperature changes as slight as 0.026 °C, and enlarged teeth at the anterior-most regions of the mouth.

TREE BOAS AND THEIR
NATURAL HISTORY

The tree boas and their family rank among the oldest of surviving snakes. It seems likely that they evolved to take advantage of the favorable environment and comparatively unexploited source of food up in the trees, and through this early divergence they have become a highly specialized group. As adaptations for climbing, the body has become elongate and laterally compressed. The tail is strongly prehensile and, in helping to subdue relatively large prey, it is wrapped securely around a branch to provide anchorage. It further enables the snake to keep a firm hold on thin branches when climbing, and is also used as an "appendage" from which the snake often suspends itself when killing and swallowing prey. One of the chief diagnostic features of the genus is the size of the anterior maxillary and mandibular teeth. These have become greatly enlarged, functioning not unlike meat hooks to reduce the risk of prey struggling free and being irretrievably lost. The posterior teeth are smaller. Tree boa heads are large, pear-shaped, covered with small scales or plates, and distinctly set off from the narrow neck. The heat-sensitive labial pits, opening between the scales, are large and well developed. Each pit is set at a slightly different angle to provide the widest possible field of reception, thus optimizing the snakes' chances of finding prey. Beneath the lower jaw there is a prominent mental groove. The small spur-like rudiments of the hind limbs are shorter in the female than in the male, a feature common to boid snakes in general. During courtship they are used by the male to "stroke" and stimulate the female while in the act of mating.

Distribution and Abundance

Species of *Corallus* are neotropical in distribution and generally favor humid forest habitats, particularly lowland river valleys. Vegetation, temperature, rainfall, and prey distribution and abundance have a bearing on the distribution and seasonal incidence of the snakes (Henderson et al., 1995). See Table 1. The habitat and trophic generalist *C. hortulanus* is widely sympatric with both *C. annulatus* and *C. caninus*, species that may have more specialized ecological requirements than *C. hortulanus*. *Corallus annulatus* and *C. caninus* would both seem to utilize the same food resources at the same time of day and in the same habitat structure, though in their geographical distribution are mutually exclusive.

Due to the secretive behavior of snakes it can be extremely difficult to establish how common, or rare as the case may be, they are in the wild. This is perhaps especially true of forest-dwelling arboreal species, such as the tree boas, for which very little information is available concerning population size and densities. Dunn (1949) provides some indication of the relative abundance of *C. hortulanus* and *C. annulatus* based on huge collections made in Panama. The Darien collection consisted of 3,044 specimens representing 44 species; *C. enydris (hortulanus)* was represented by 346 specimens (the third most common species) and *C. annulatus* by 1. Similarly, the Yavisa sample (a subsample of the Darien collection), taken in the years 1933–1937, consisted of 2,321 snakes of which 171 were *C. enydris*

Table 1. Latitudinal range, altitudinal range, number of vegetation/edaphic zones (based on Campbell and Lamar, 1989), and morphoclimatic domains (Ab'Saber, 1977) occupied by each species of *Corallus* on the neotropical mainland, and number of islands occupied by each species (Henderson et al., 1995).

	Latitudinal Range (degrees)	Altitudinal Range (m)	Vegetation/Edaphic Zones	Morphoclimatic Domains	No. of Islands in Distribution
Corallus annulatus	19	0–400	1	3	0
Corallus caninus	24	0–1000	2	2	0
Corallus cropanii	1	0–50	1	1	0
Corallus hortulanus	38	0–1000	8	9	19

(*hortulanus*) but only 1 *C. annulatus*, a species that, although fairly wide-ranging, would seem to be nowhere common. Henderson and Winstel (1992) and Henderson (unpubl.) determined population densities of *C. hortulanus* on Grenada based on direct counts and mark-recapture: their estimates ranged from 19 to 51 snakes per hectare. Henderson and Henderson (1995) calculated encounter rates of *C. hortulanus* at different altitudes and habitats on Grenada: at low elevations (50 m above sea level or lower) the rate was 4.5 snakes/hour; at moderate elevations (50–400 m), 3.0 snakes/hour; and at high elevations (greater than 400 m) it was 0.2 snake/hour.

Finding and Catching Prey

Tree boas are essentially crepuscular and nocturnal in habits, remaining inactive during the day concealed among dense foliage or out of sight in holes or crevices in large trees. When exposed, they rely on immobility and their cryptic coloration to avoid detection by predators. They are for the most part opportunistic in their feeding habits, preying on frogs, lizards, birds, and small mammals (including bats). Birds may be captured as they alight to roost or actively hunted at night; they are located by olfactory, thermal, and visual cues. Henderson (1988) described the foraging behavior of a large *C. hortulanus* in the canopy of a tree. He observed the snake moving slowly through the foliage and every foot or so lower the forepart of its body, apparently to investigate what was below, and then after a short while resume crawling through the branches. After having made its way to the other side of the tree it would then reverse and hunt through a higher or lower part of the canopy, periodically lowering its head in the same way.

When prey is located, the snake becomes highly alert, approaching the unsuspecting animal slowly and stealthily with rapid protrusions of the tongue. Stalking may to some extent be initiated by prey movement. As the snake closes to within a

Figure 2.   Common tree boa (*C. hortulanus*) swallowing prey. Food is held securely in the coils and usually swallowed while the snake hangs suspended from a branch, anchored by its lower body and prehensile tail. Drawing by Peter J. Stafford.

distance of twenty centimeters or so, it draws the body up into an S-shaped loop, and then strikes, immediately grasping the animal and overpowering it in its coils. When captured, the animal is asphyxiated by constriction and usually swallowed head first (Figure 2). In case it should fall and be lost to the ground below, it is never released and always held securely in the coils. If the strike should be unsuccessful, the snake does not follow in pursuit, but, in its disorientated state, remains still and investigates the spot where the animal had previously been.

In the wild it is probable that the snakes obtain moisture by drinking rainwater that collects on their coils, or from droplets on vegetation, or possibly from the reservoir vases of epiphytic bromeliads.

Enemies and Defense

The principal enemies of tree boas are probably birds of prey, but it is likely that they are also caught and eaten by small carnivorous mammals (Henderson et al., 1996). In the early stages of life there may be significant mortality among juveniles through predation and possibly failure to capture sufficient food. The snakes themselves are host to a number of internal and external parasites, including mites, ticks and nematode worms of various kinds, but in nature do not appear to suffer seriously from heavy infestation.

With the possible exception of *C. cropanii*, tree boas all tend to be rather aggressive by nature, and if provoked at close quarters will defend themselves vigorously, coiling and striking repeatedly. *Corallus hortulanus* will also "rattle" its tail against surrounding vegetation.

It may be common for tree boas to be mobbed by birds or primates should they be found moving about during daylight. The behavior of a family group of Saddle-back tamarins (*Saguinus fuscicollis nigrifons*) in Peru mobbing a pair of *C. hortulanus* is described by Bartecki and Heymann (1987). Upon finding the snakes hanging from a liana, apparently mating, the tamarins started to emit excitement calls, but although two individuals approached to within 1.5 to 2 meters, they were not observed to physically attack the snakes. Henderson et al. (1996) and Henderson and Winstel (1995) have also noted the molestation of *C. hortulanus* by the introduced primate *Cercopithecus mona* on Grenada.

Mating and Reproduction

In common with other boids, reproduction in tree boas would seem to be related to seasonal climatic changes, with mating tending to take place mainly between the months of December and April. Mating usually takes place among tree branches at night. The male courts the female by repeatedly crawling over her and rapidly vibrating his spurs upon the lateral and dorsal areas of her body, while at the same time continuously flicking his tongue. This is followed by tail-search movements, wrapping the tail around the posterior part of the female's body and attempting to copulate; this may continue for several hours before mating finally takes place. After mating the snakes resume a solitary existence. In common with other boas, the tree boas produce living young and have fairly large broods for arboreal snake species. The snakes of this genus are by nature slow-moving and, although well adapted for movement in the trees, they are rather inept on the ground.

From observations in captivity, the gestation period of *Corallus* species varies on average between 180 and 250 days; during the later stages of which the female does not usually feed and often spends a great deal of time basking. Prior to giving birth she sheds her skin. Parturition may take several hours, and almost immediately after they are born the neonate snakes break free from their ovicular membranes and begin to disperse, instinctively climbing upwards through the surrounding vegetation. During the first days of life they subsist on a food reserve of egg yolk, and later begin to feed on small lizards, nestling birds, and small rodents.

Key to the Species and Diagnoses of Species and Subspecies of the Genus *Corallus*

Definition

In general habitus, species of *Corallus* are boids with laterally compressed bodies (only slightly so in *C. cropanii*), anterior maxillary teeth extremely long, some labials with deep pits, large chunky heads, strongly prehensile tails (*C. cropanii* may be an exception), and exhibiting little sexual dimorphism (to date, only males are known in *C. cropanii*) in traditional meristic characters. Dorsal scales are in 29–77 rows at midbody, ventrals 179–294, and subcaudals 51–141. Some supralabials and infralabials have deep pits. Dorsal ground color is extremely variable, ranging through yellow, red-orange, red-brown, tan, khaki, beige, milk chocolate-brown, dark brown, taupe, gray, bright green, olive green, and gray-green. Dorsally, snakes may be patternless to heavily patterned with small flecks, rhombs or some modification of a rhomboidal shape, hourglasses, spades, or small triangles; pattern elements have either angular or rounded edges. The ventral ground color is white, cream, beige, bright yellow, or

17

dull yellow. The venter may be immaculate to heavily patterned, and the posterior portion of the venter is almost invariably more heavily patterned than the anterior portion.

Diagnosis

Corallus is characterized by a combination of long, gently curved anterior maxillary teeth, labial scales with deep pits in many of them, and the upper labials are separated from the orbit. *Epicrates cenchria* has long, curved anterior maxillary teeth, shallow labial pits, and the upper labials enter the orbit. Subcaudals in all species of *Corallus* except *C. cropanii* are usually greater than 65, but usually less than 65 in *E. cenchria*. *Corallus cropanii* has fewer than 40 dorsal scale rows at midbody, whereas *E. cenchria* has more than 40. No other New World boine can be confused with any species of *Corallus*.

Distribution

Species of *Corallus* are found on the neotropical mainland from Honduras to southeastern Brazil (just south of the Tropic of Capricorn). Insular distribution (*C. hortulanus* only) includes islands off the Atlantic and Pacific coasts of Panama, Isla Margarita, Trinidad, Tobago, the West Indian islands of St. Vincent, several of the Grenadines, and Grenada, and Ilha Grande off southeastern Brazil.

Key to the Species of *Corallus*

1. Dorsal scale rows at midbody fewer than 35; subcaudals fewer than 60 in males (females unknown) .... *C. cropanii*
   Dorsal scale rows at midbody greater than 35; subcaudals greater than 65 2

2. Nasals usually not in contact; subcaudals 65–87 3
   Nasals almost always in contact; subcaudals 99–141; dorsal scale
   rows at midbody 37–63; ventrals 250–294; loreolabials usually in
   2 rows (rarely 3); dorsal ground color variable (yellow, red-
   orange, red-brown, dark brown, taupe, gray) ..... *C. hortulanus*
3. Dorsal scale rows at midbody 50–57; ventrals 251–268;
   subcaudals 79–87; dorsal ground color red-brown, red-orange,
   brown, or taupe .... *C. annulatus*
   Dorsal scale rows at midbody 63–77; ventrals 186–209;
   subcaudals 65–74; dorsal ground color yellow to red-brown in
   juveniles and green in adults; usually with white dorsal
   markings .... *C. caninus*

Diagnoses

Corallus annulatus (Cope)

Corallus annulatus is most easily confused with *C. hortulanus*. In
C. annulatus the nasals are usually not in contact and there are
79–87 subcaudals; in *C. hortulanus*, the nasals are usually in
contact and there are 99–141 subcaudals. In *C. caninus*, dorsal
scales at midbody are in 63–77 rows and in *C. cropanii* they are
in fewer than 35 rows; in *C. annulatus*, midbody dorsal scale
rows are 50–57.

Corallus annulatus annulatus

Corallus annulatus was characterized by Rendahl and Vestergren
(1940, 1941) by the presence of one pair of internasals; anterior
lateral internasals are in contact and the posterior lateral internasals are separated by a single median scale. These characters are of dubious diagnostic value. The number of supraloreals, a character suggested by Peters (1957) as possibly
having some diagnostic value, is also too variable to be useful.
See the Diagnosis for *C. a. blombergi*.

Corallus annulatus blombergi (Rendahl and Vestergren)

Corallus a. blombergi was characterized by Rendahl and Vester-gren (1941) by the presence of one pair of internasals and two lateral internasals separated by two median scales arranged one behind the other. This is a variable character and of little diagnostic value. This subspecies is better diagnosed by dorsal ground color and pattern, and by several other scale characters. Dorsal ground color usually milk chocolate-brown to rich dark brown (opposed to beige or red-brown in most Central American and Colombian snakes); dorsal blotches 7–9 scales wide at midbody, each with a central area that is paler than the dorsal ground color (as opposed to dorsal blotches 8–12 scales wide at midbody, each with a central area that is more or less the same shade as the dorsal ground color). *Corallus a. blombergi* has 6 loreals + subloreals as opposed to 6–12 in Central American and Colombian specimens.

Corallus annulatus colombianus (Rendahl and Vestergren)

Corallus a. colombianus was characterized by Rendahl and Vester-gren (1940, 1941) by the presence of one pair of internasals and a pair of large lateral internasals in contact anteriorly, but separated posteriorly by a single median internasal. This is a character of dubious value, but so few specimens of *C. a. colombianus* are available that it is not possible to determine the presence of characters of greater diagnostic value. It is likely that *C. a. colombianus* should be placed in synonymy with *C. a. annulatus*.

Corallus caninus (Linnaeus)

Corallus caninus is characterized 186–218 ventrals, compared to more than 250 in *C. annulatus* and *C. hortulanus*. It has 62–84 dorsal scale rows at midbody, compared to 37–57 in *C. annulatus* and *C. hortulanus*. *Corallus cropanii*, the sister species of *C. caninus* (Kluge, 1991), has only 29–32 dorsal scale rows at midbody. Juvenile (yellow) *C. caninus* bear a superficial resemblance to the yellow phase *C. hortulanus*, but scale characters easily distinguish the two taxa.

Corallus cropanii (Hoge)

Corallus cropanii may be distinguished from all other neotropical boines by the low number of dorsal scale rows at midbody (29–32). *Corallus caninus*, the species most similar to *C. cropanii*, has more than 60; *C. hortulanus* from southeastern Brazil has more than 50. *Epicrates cenchria* in southern Brazil has more than 40 dorsal scale rows at midbody.

Corallus hortulanus (Linnaeus)

Corallus hortulanus usually has nasals in contact (usually not in contact in *C. annulatus* and *C. caninus*); *C. hortulanus* has 99–133 subcaudals compared to 79–87 in *C. annulatus*, 65–74 in *C. caninus*, and fewer than 60 in *C. cropanii*. Juvenile (yellow) *C. caninus* bear a superficial resemblance to yellow phase *C. hortulanus*, but scale characters easily distinguish the two taxa.

Corallus hortulanus hortulanus

Corallus h. hortulanus is best characterized by 50 or more dorsal scale rows at midbody (rarely a specimen will have 47 or 48 in Peru or Bolivia); *C. h. cooki* invariably has fewer than 50.

Corallus hortulanus cooki (Gray)

Corallus h. cooki is best characterized by having fewer than 50 dorsal scale rows at midbody (as opposed to 50 or more in *C. h. hortulanus*). The number of dorsal scale rows changes in a very short distance along the body of *C. hortulanus*. On the South American mainland, the primary element in the dorsal pattern usually has rounded edges in *C. h. hortulanus* and a rhombic shape with sharper edges in *C. h. cooki*. Some specimens from the south bank of the Río Orinoco in northeastern Venezuela exhibit a combination of fewer than 50 midbody dorsal scale rows and rounded pattern elements at midbody. Snakes with less than 50 and more than 50 midbody dorsal scale rows occur in coastal Guyana and Suriname, and possibly coastal French Guiana (Chippaux, 1986). Although *C. h. hortulanus* exhibits mean differences in a number of characters (e.g., ventrals, number of scales between supraorbitals, number of loreolabials), there is considerable overlap in these characters which make them of limited diagnostic value.

Plate 1. *Boa constrictor* from Lomalinda, Meta, Colombia. Photograph by William W. Lamar.

Plate 2. *Epicrates cenchria* from Vaupés, Colombia. Photograph by William W. Lamar.

Plate 3. Common anaconda, *Eunectes murinus,* from Ilha de Maracá, Roraima, Brazil. Photograph by Mark O'Shea.

Plate 4. Head of a Common anaconda (*Eunectes murinus*) from Orinduik, Guyana. Photograph by Mark O'Shea.

Plate 5. *Sanzinia madagascariensis* (male), the tree boa of Madagascar. Although once placed in the same genus as the neotropical tree boas, cladistic analysis suggests it is more closely related to *Acrantophis,* the other boine genus of Madagascar, and *Boa constrictor* of Latin America. Photograph by Peter J. Stafford.

Plate 6. Common tree boa (*Corallus hortulanus*), from St. Andrew Parish, Grenada (elevation 30 meters). Photograph by Robert W. Henderson.

Plate 7. Common tree boa (*Corallus hortulanus*), from Grenada (elevation 30 meters). Photograph by Robert W. Henderson.

Plate 8. Common tree boa (*Corallus hortulanus*), from Grenada (elevation 30 meters). Photograph by R. Allan Winstel.

Plate 9. Habitat of *Corallus hortulanus* in the Vermont Nature Reserve on St. Vincent, West Indies. Photograph by Rose M. Henderson.

Plate 10. A female Common tree boa (*Corallus hortulanus*) from 210 meters elevation, St. Patrick Parish, St. Vincent, Lesser Antilles. Photograph by Robert W. Henderson.

Plate 11. *Corallus hortulanus* from St. David Parish, Grenada (elevation 65 meters). Photograph by R. Allan Winstel.

Plate 12. A small *Corallus hortulanus* being hooked out of a tree at Hollis Reservoir, Trinidad. Photograph by Kirsten Kranz.

Plate 13. *Corallus hortulanus* from Grenada on a banana flower spike (elevation 270 meters). It is not uncommon for these snakes to "sit-and-wait" among flowers or bunches of ripening fruit and ambush small animals that may approach to feed. Photograph by Rose M. Henderson.

Plate 14. *Corallus hortulanus* from St. Andrew Parish, Grenada (elevation 457 meters). Photograph by Robert W. Henderson.

Plate 15. Habitat of *Corallus hortulanus* in an area of mixed agriculture in St. David Parish, Grenada. Photograph by R. Allan Winstel.

Plate 16. Radio-locating a *Corallus hortulanus* along the Beausejour River in Grenada. Photograph by R. Allan Winstel.

Plate 17. Adult female "black-tailed" Common tree boa (*Corallus hortulanus*), typical of the color variety "ruschenbergerii" described as a separate species by Cope in 1876. Photograph by Peter J. Stafford.

Plate 18. A juvenile Common tree boa (*Corallus hortulanus*), born from the snake illustrated in Plate 17. Specimens of this color morph develop a conspicuous black tail with age. Photograph by Peter J. Stafford.

Plate 19. *Corallus hortulanus* from Hollis Reservoir, Northern Range, Trinidad, illustrating the heat-sensitive labial pits. Photograph by Robert W. Henderson.

Plate 20. *Corallus hortulanus* from Hollis Reservoir, Northern Range, Trinidad. Photograph by Hans E. A. Boos.

Plate 21. *Corallus hortulanus* from Puerto Porfía, Meta, Colombia. Photograph by William W. Lamar.

Plate 22. *Corallus hortulanus* from Río Matiyure, Apure, Venezuela. Photograph by William F. Holmstrom.

Plate 23. *Corallus hortulanus* from Apoteri, Guyana. Photograph by Mark O'Shea.

Plate 24. *Corallus hortulanus* from the Lower Río Yarape, Loreto, Peru. Photograph by William W. Lamar.

Plate 25. *Corallus hortulanus* from the Lower Río Yarape, Loreto, Peru. Photograph by William W. Lamar.

Plate 26. Dry *terra-firme* forest, Maracá, Roraima, Brazil. A cleared trail and typical habitat of *Corallus hortulanus*. At dusk the snakes position themselves on branches at the side of the trail waiting for the opportunity to capture bats flying up and down in search of food. Photograph by Mark O'Shea.

Plate 27

Plates 27, 28, 29, 30. Four color forms of the Common tree boa (*Corallus hortulanus*), all taken from branches along the same trail through *terra-firme* forest in Maracá, Roraima, Brazil. Photographs by Mark O'Shea.

Plate 28

Plate 29

Plate 30

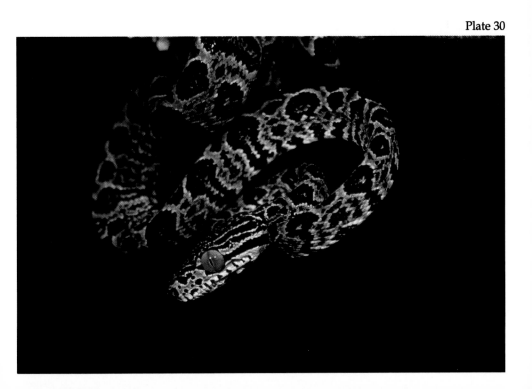

Plate 31. A Brazilian specimen of *Corallus hortulanus* with an unusually dark, pink-colored venter. Photograph by Mark O'Shea.

Plate 32. *Corallus hortulanus* from Manaus, Amazonas, Brazil. Photograph by Mark O'Shea.

Plate 33. *Corallus hortulanus* from Marcílio Dias, Santa Catarina, Brazil (26° 08′ S latitude). Photograph by Giuseppe Puorto.

Plate 34. Juvenile *Corallus caninus* from Tucuri, Para, Brazil. Photograph by Giuseppe Puorto.

Plate 35. *Corallus caninus* from Porto Velho, Rondônia, Brazil, illustrating the ontogenetic change of color from brown to green. Photograph by Giuseppe Puorto.

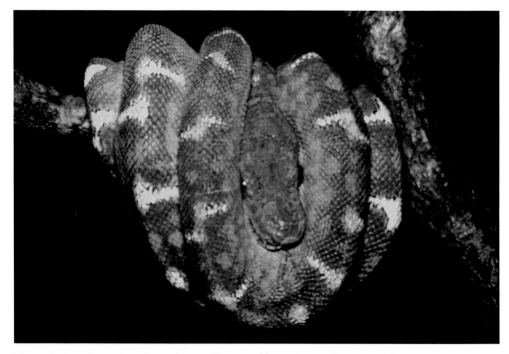

Plate 36. *Corallus caninus* from Porto Velho, Rondônia, Brazil, illustrating the ontogenetic change of color from brown to green. Photograph by Giuseppe Puorto.

Plate 37. Adult *Corallus caninus* from the vicinity of Ariquemes, Rondônia, Brazil. Photograph by W. Carl Taylor.

Plate 38. Adult female *Corallus caninus* from Porto Alegre do Norte, Mato Grosso, Brazil. Photograph by Giuseppe Puorto.

Plate 39. The Green tree python, *Morelia (= Chondropython) viridis* of northern Australia and New Guinea (this individual from Riwo, Madang, Papua New Guinea). A remarkably similar species to the Emerald tree boa, both in its appearance and behavior. Photograph by Mark O'Shea.

Plate 40. The Annulated tree boa (*Corallus annulatus*) in its most usual color form (juvenile). Photograph by Richard S. Reed.

Plate 41

Plates 41, 42, 43. Three different color forms (adult) of the Annulated tree boa (*Corallus annulatus*), captive bred from parents collected in Limón Province, Costa Rica. Photographs by Richard S. Reed.

Plate 42

Plate 43

Plate 44. An unusual piebald color form of *Corallus annulatus*. This individual was born with the normal color and markings of the species, losing pigment as it grew older. Photograph by Richard S. Reed.

Plate 45. A colorful form of the Annulated tree boa (*Corallus annulatus*). Photograph by Richard S. Reed.

Plate 46. *Corallus annulatus* from Guayacán de Turrialba, Costa Rica (elevation about 400 meters). Photograph by William W. Lamar.

Plate 47. A captive male "orange-eyed" Common tree boa (*Corallus hortulanus cooki*). Photograph by Peter J. Stafford.

Plate 48. A captive-bred young Common tree boa (*Corallus hortulanus hortulanus*). Photograph by R. Allan Winstel.

Plate 49. Male parent *Corallus caninus* of neonates illustrated in Plates 50 and 51. Photograph by Peter J. Stafford.

Plate 50. A captive-bred neonate Emerald tree boa at 23 days old. Photograph by Peter J. Stafford.

Plate 51. Captive-bred Emerald tree boa (female) showing the extent of green pigment development at 2 years of age. Photograph by Peter J. Stafford.

Plate 52. Many breeders of *Corallus caninus* advocate keeping newborn neonates separately in individual "sweet jars" with water in the bottom to maintain high humidity. The jars have lids fitted with fine mesh for ventilation and are all stacked together in a large, heated container. Photograph by Peter J. Stafford.

Plate 53. A simply furnished rearing unit, using absorbent paper or similar, easily changed substrate, is the most widely preferred way of maintaining captive tree boas. Photograph by Peter J. Stafford.

THE COMMON TREE BOA
(*Corallus hortulanus*)

This is the most common, geographically widespread, and well-known of the tree boas, and there can be few other snake species anywhere in the world that occur in such an extraordinarily wide range of color patterns. There are two subspecies: the nominate race, most frequently called the Garden or Amazon tree boa, and Cook's tree boa (*C. hortulanus cooki*), though together these snakes are known under a collection of other, largely meaningless, names which reflect their various color patterns, such as Brown tree boa, Red tree boa, Yellow-marbled tree boa and Orange-eyed tree boa. The species also has many other regional names, such as *Macaurel, Oroya* and *Falsa mapanare dormilona* (Venezuela), *Cobra de veado, Cobra veadeira, Suauboia* (Amazonian Brazil), *Sarpint* (Grenada), *Congo Snake* (St. Vincent), *Cascabel* (Trinidad and Tobago) and *Ya-mung* (Akawai Indian, Guyana). Extreme color forms of this boa have on more than one occasion been mistakenly described as separate species. The Common tree boa is illustrated in Plates 6–33.

Etymology

The specific name *hortulanus* is from the Latin for "gardener". Linnaeus described the head pattern of *Boa hortulana* as having golden-yellow splotches and resembling a garden. Subsequently, Shaw (1802) coined the name "garden boa" for the species. It is therefore coincidence that the species exhibits a strong proclivity for agricultural areas (e.g., fruit orchards). The name *cooki* is a patronym given in honor of Edward Cook, who is deemed to have found or donated what then became the type specimen.

Geographic Range

Corallus hortulanus has an extensive distribution in the Neotropics. It occurs from southwestern Costa Rica (south of 10° N) and through Panama (including Isla del Rey, Isla Contadora, Isla de Cébaco, Isla Suscantupu). In South American it is found in Colombia (east of the Andes, although Pérez-Santos and Moreno [1988] note specimens from west of the Andes), Venezuela (including Isla Margarita) and through Guyana, Suriname, and French Guiana. It occurs in Amazonian Ecuador, Peru, and Bolivia. In Brazil, *C. hortulanus* is encountered south of the Tropic of Capricorn to 26° 08' in the state of São Paulo, and also on Ilha Grande off the southeast coast. Insular distribution includes Trinidad and Tobago, and in the West Indies it is known from St. Vincent, many of the Grenadines (Bequia, Isle Quarte, Baliceaux, Mustique, Canouan, Mayreau, Union, Carriacou, Petit Martinique), and Grenada. Altitudinal distribution is from sea level to about 1000 m. The distribution of *C. h. hortulanus* is largely coincident with the distribution of lowland tropical rain forest and it is virtually absent from typical caatinga in eastern Brazil, but it does occur in areas peripheral and/or transitional to caatinga (Puorto and Henderson, 1994); in general, it is absent from areas that receive less than 1500 mm of precipitation annually. It does occur in Atlantic coastal forest in southern Brazil. *Corallus h. cooki* occurs in a wider range of habitats (from cactus and thorn scrub to rain forest) and rainfall regimes, including areas that receive less than 1000 mm of precipitation annually (Henderson et al., 1995).

Description

Maximum SVL is at least 1870 mm (from Trinidad). The general habitus is that of a large chunky head, long anterior maxillary teeth, slender neck, strongly laterally compressed body, and prehensile tail. Few snake species show greater color pattern variation than *C. hortulanus*. Following are color pattern descriptions from five geographic areas (some very broad) that describe some of the remarkable variability in this species.

St. Vincent

Maximum SVL is at least 1374 mm. Dorsal ground color is gray, taupe, or brown, always with a conspicuous dorsal (= lateral because of strong lateral compression) pattern; the main elements of gray or brown hourglass shapes or round-cornered rhomboid-like shapes. The venter is usually heavily patterned with dark brown.

Grenada Bank

Maximum SVL is at least 1625 mm. On Grenada, the dorsal ground color is extremely variable, including shades of yellow, orange, red, gray, taupe, brown (to nearly black), and olive. For snakes in which the dorsal ground color is yellowish, the dorsum may be completely devoid of pattern, lightly patterned with flecks of brown that occupy less than a single scale, or have a pattern of dark flecks providing the indication of an hourglass shape. Snakes that have a dorsal ground color other than yellow exhibit tremendous variability in pattern shape (anteroposteriorly elongated, dorsoventrally broadened rhomb, hourglass, spade). Dull yellow is the predominant ventral ground color, but occasionally it is cream or white. The ventral pattern may be almost immaculate, marked with flecks and spots, large blotches, or nearly covered with dark brown. The ventral pattern usually becomes denser from anterior to posterior. On the islands of the Grenadines, yellow snakes have been collected on Bequia and Union. Elsewhere dorsal ground color is gray, taupe, some shade of brown, or bright red-orange (Mayreau only). The dorsal pattern is variable, but usually some rhomboid derivative, spade, or hourglass shape.

Costa Rica, Panama (and associated islands), and Northern Colombia (north of the Cordillera Oriental)

Maximum SVL is at least 1665 mm. Dorsal ground color is yellowish, taupe, gray or some shade of brown (browns predominate). The dorsal pattern is usually a series of large rhombs, and snakes from this geographic area show more consistency than elsewhere in the shape of the main dorsal element. The ventral ground color is usually dull yellow, and may be nearly immaculate to heavily patterned (if patterned, more so on the posterior portion of the body).

Trinidad, Tobago, Isla Margarita, and Northern Venezuela

Snakes from this area tend to be very large (especially from Trinidad and the Orinoco Delta), and maximum SVL is at least 1857 mm. The dorsal ground color is yellow, yellow-brown, khaki-brown, or copper-brown. A distinct dorsal pattern may be absent, faint or conspicuous rhombs may be present, or the free edge of the dorsal scales may be edged in dark brown. The venter may be whitish, cream, dull yellow, or bright yellow, and may be immaculate to heavily marked with dark brown to black (becoming more predominant posteriorly).

Amazonia, Guianas, and Atlantic Rain Forest

Maximum SVL is at least 1640 mm. Dorsal ground color may be yellow with some shade of brown or gray, but taupe is the predominant color. A dorsal pattern may be absent (if the dorsal ground color is yellow), but usually it is a dorsoventrally elongated rhomboidal shape, distinct or not, gray, taupe, or brown in color. The venter may be white, cream, or (predominantly) dull yellow; it may be immaculate, have a few flecks, scattered spots and blotches, or be nearly completely covered with dark brown. The ventral pattern becomes heavier posteriorly.

Corallus hortulanus exhibits virtually no sexual dimorphism in pertinent scale characters. Ranges in meristic features are as follows: dorsal scale rows at midbody 37–63; ventrals 250–294; subcaudals 94–133; ventrals + subcaudals 351–436; supralabials (with well-developed labial pits) 8–14; infralabials (with well-developed labial pits) 11–17; scales between supraorbitals 3–14; loreals 1–4; subloreals 0–9; loreals + subloreals 1–11; circumorbital series 9–17; nasals usually in contact with 4–14 scales bordering nasals. The hemipenis in a *C. h. hortulanus* (from Venezuela south of the Río Orinoco) is 19 mm long and undivided, the arms reduced to terminal lateral bulges. The sulcus divides 10 mm from the base and the forks run centrifugally to the tips of the lateral bulges; sulcal folds large, slightly raised and unadorned; ornamentation flounced; proximal third of organ nude, followed distally by three shallow, transverse flounces that fuse with the sulcal folds and encircle the organ. Two rows of coarse papillae (derived from papillate flounces) encircle the organ, and the distal quarter of the organ is covered with scattered, shallow, rounded papillae (Branch, 1981). In comparison (only differences, not similarities, are noted), in *C. h. cooki* (from Panama), the hemipenis is 34 mm long and shallowly forked (crotch at 32 mm). The sulcus divides 20 mm from the base; the sulcal folds are not raised. The basal quarter of the organ is nude, distally encircled by five well-developed wavy flounces (fused with the sulcal fold and occurring proximad to the sulcal furcation), chevron-shaped with apices directed dorsally on the asulcal surface; the most proximal flounce extended into a small basal papilla on asulcal surface. The remainder of the organ is covered by many scattered, rounded papillae that are smaller on the arms; small scattered papillae also occur between prominent basal flounces, particularly on the asulcate surface (Branch, 1981).

Henderson and Hedges (1995), utilizing mitochondrial DNA sequences of samples from seven geographically disparate localities, provided evidence of phylogenetic relationships in *Corallus hortulanus*. The monophyly of *C. hortulanus* was cor-

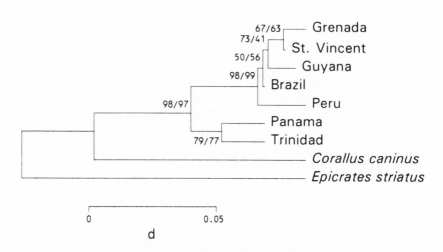

Figure 3. Phylogenetic relationships of *Corallus hortulanus* from seven widely distributed localities, inferred from a neighbor-joining analysis of DNA sequences (Jukes-Cantor distance) of a portion of the mitochondrial cytochrome b gene. The numbers on the tree are statistical estimates of confidence of each node: the "confidence probability" (Rzhetsky and Nei., 1992; Kumar et al., 1993) derived from the standard error estimate of the branch length (left of slash), and the bootstrap P-value (Felsenstein, 1985) based on 2000 replications (right). The West Indian boine species *Epicrates striatus* was used to root the tree. d = distance. Modified from Henderson and Hedges (1995).

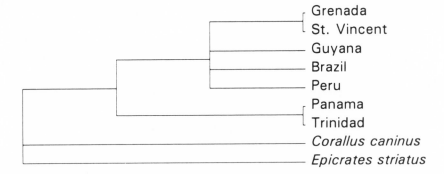

Figure 4. Phylogenetic relationships of *Corallus hortulanus* inferred from a maximum parsimony analysis (branch-and-bound). The tree is a strict consensus of six most-parsimonious trees, each of length = 41. Modified from Henderson and Hedges (1995).

roborated and a major dichotomy between northern samples (Panama and Trinidad) and southern samples was found, corresponding to the two currently recognized subspecies (Figures 3 and 4). Unexpectedly, the samples from St. Vincent and Grenada (currently assigned to *C. h. cooki*) cluster with the southern (assigned to *C. h. hortulanus*) rather than the geographically closer northern samples (e.g., Trinidad). The results imply a fairly recent (Quaternary; Hedges, 1996) Guianan-Amazonian origin of West Indian populations. Henderson and Hedges (1995), noting that *C. hortulanus* reached the West Indies by overwater dispersal from South America, suggested it was plausible for *C. hortulanus* to have reached the West Indies from northeastern Brazil or the Guianas via the South Equatorial Current.

The range of colors and patterns exhibited in this snake is bewildering and there would appear to be almost as many different combinations of colors as there are individuals. The fact that entirely different color morphs can be found living together is some indication of the high degree of polymorphism, and it is not unusual to find an assortment of differently colored neonates within a single brood (Stafford, 1986). Various attempts have been made to explain and classify them. Boulenger (1893) described four main color types previously considered to be separate species. However, while certain color varieties predominate in some areas, there does not seem to be any consistent pattern in the distribution of color forms across this snake's range. Recent research, however, has shown that the different phases may to some extent be selectively distributed according to certain environmental factors.

The basic dorsal color of *C. hortulanus* ranges from various shades of yellow, orange, red, or brown to gray or olive green, with or without a pattern or flecks of darker and paler pigmentation. Snakes from Trinidad, Tobago, Isla Margarita, and northern Venezuela frequently lack dorsal markings and tend to be larger in size. Where pattern is concerned, the lateral markings of *C. h. hortulanus* are described as more rounded than those of *C. h. cooki*, though this is not a particularly reliable character and would seldom seem to apply.

Extensive field studies by Henderson (1990a, b) on Grenada indicate that the different colors and patterns of *C. hortulanus*, in at least some parts of the West Indies, appear to be correlated with altitude and rainfall (Figure 5), the snakes falling into one of four main categories: yellow (yellow-brown, khaki, tan); red (brick-red, brownish red); taupe (gray-brown, gray); and dark brown. Moreover, while each form occurs in some numbers virtually everywhere, certain categories predominated at particular altitudes and in different rainfall regimes: (1) Snakes that were pale in coloration (yellow, khaki, pale brown, etc.) predominated in areas that were close to sea level, received a depressed amount of annual precipitation, and many hours of sunlight/day. (2) With increasing altitude and rainfall (and, therefore, cloud cover) and a corresponding decrease in mean ambient temperature and hours of sunlight/day, the number of "yellow" snakes declined and taupe, gray, and darker shades of brown became more predominant. (3) At the highest elevations, *C. hortulanus* was predominantly dark brown, ambient temperature and the number of hours of sunlight/day were

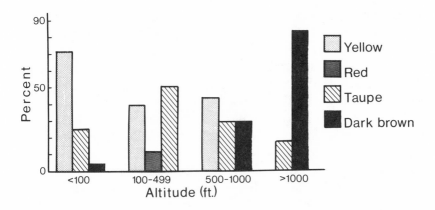

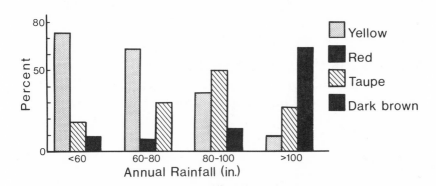

Figure 5. The percentages at which four different predominant dorsal color categories occurred in a sample of 66 *Corallus hortulanus* collected on Grenada at four different altitudinal ranges (upper) and four different rainfall regimes (lower). From Henderson, 1990b.

depressed, and rainfall and cloud cover were excessive. Henderson and Henderson (1995) found a similar relationship and correlated it with body temperature.

With ascending altitude and increasing precipitation, the shape of the dorsal pattern of the snakes also becomes less angular and more rounded in shape with yellow snakes being patternless or having rhomboid markings, and darker colored snakes being more heavily marked. This strongly suggests that the distribution of color morphs on Grenada is, at least to some extent, related to thermoregulation, particularly at altitudes where the cooler temperatures and longer periods of cloud cover would be naturally conducive to the survival of dark-colored snakes. Similar color forms to those found in Grenada are known to occur throughout the range of *C. hortulanus*, although not with such frequency. A yellow-colored snake, recently recorded from a locality in southern Brazil (Puorto and Henderson, 1994), suggests that thermoregulation may perhaps not have a bearing on the distribution of color forms over the species' range as a whole. This particular individual was found in an area of seasonally depressed temperature.

Longevity

A wild-caught *C. h. hortulanus* of adult size (sex unknown) at the St. Louis Zoo lived in captivity for 10 years and 4 months, and a wild-caught adult female *C. h. cooki* at the San Diego Zoo is known to have lived for 14 years and 3 months (Bowler, 1977).

Ecological Data

Habitat

The biotope of *C. hortulanus* varies widely, and the species occurs in a more diverse range of habitats and is more adaptable than any of its congeners. It can be found in lowland primary forest, secondary rain forest, dry *terra-firme* woodland, palmetto-savanna, *Acacia*-cactus scrub, mangroves, and swamp forest. In particular, these boas seem to favor woodland edge situations and trees and shrubs overhanging water, but have also been found living in caves and around human habitation, even venturing into the roofs of houses. Some of the densest populations in the West Indies occur in or adjacent to fruit orchards, espe-

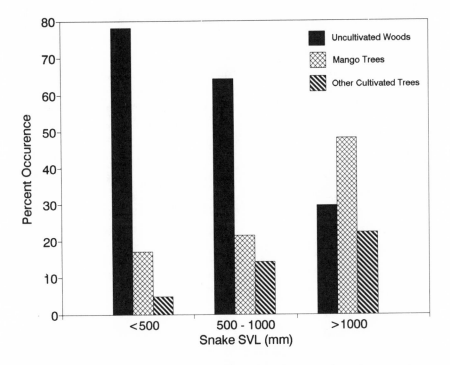

Figure 6. Percent occurrence of three size classes of *Corallus hortulanus* in three habitat types in an area of mixed agriculture on Grenada (modified from Henderson and Winstel, 1995)

cially mango, but also breadfruit, cacao, nutmeg, coconut, lime, and banana groves, where prey animals may occur in greater numbers due to the abundance of food. A study (Henderson and Winstel, 1995) of habitat selection by *Corallus hortulanus* in an area of mixed agriculture on Grenada (Figure 6) indicated that contiguous tree crowns were the single most important habitat criterion: 200 of 201 observations (99.5%) were made while snakes were in trees or bushes that were in contact with other trees or bushes. Tree boas were encountered routinely in tree lines only one tree wide and usually with a high incidence of mango or breadfruit trees (and often bordering small plots of sugarcane). Tree boa SVL was positively correlated with distance from the distal portion of the occupied branch, perch height, and perch diameter. Of these three perch characters, perch diameter was most important in separating size classes of *C. hortulanus*.

In its natural habitat *C. hortulanus* can be approached and captured during daylight with ease but reacts viciously when seized, lashing the body and occasionally startling its captor by "rattling" its tail against surrounding foliage. The snakes usually spend the day coiled in a tight "ball" at the distal end of a branch, anywhere from 2 to 25 meters high in a tree, sometimes completely exposed. At night they can often be located by the reflection of their eyes, which shine orange-red in the beam of a light visible from over 40 meters away. This is caused by the light being reflected back by a mirroring device called the *tapetum lucidum* (Walls, 1942).

Foraging and Diet

In the West Indies, *Corallus hortulanus* becomes active at dusk (ca. 1800 h). Activity tapers off after 2400 h, but some activity may continue until daybreak (Henderson and Winstel, 1992). In Guiana their period of activity has been recorded from approximately 1700 to 0600 hours. On Grenada, body temperatures of foraging tree boas vary with altitude. Near sea level, mean body temperature of the nocturnally foraging snakes was 25.6 °C; at moderate elevations (50–400 m) it was 24.1 °C; and at high elevations (above 400 m) it was 22.8 °C. Not surprisingly, body temperature of the foraging tree boas was correlated with ambient (air) temperature, but the number of snakes with body temperature above air temperature was significant (Henderson and Henderson, 1995).

Common tree boas employ both active and ambush foraging modes. Snakes that are of a size class that feeds predominantly on sleeping lizards and birds must actively search for their prey. Conversely, tree boas that are of a size class that preys on rodents may employ a sit-and-wait mode to ambush nocturnally active rodents. Of 230 observations of foraging tree boas in the

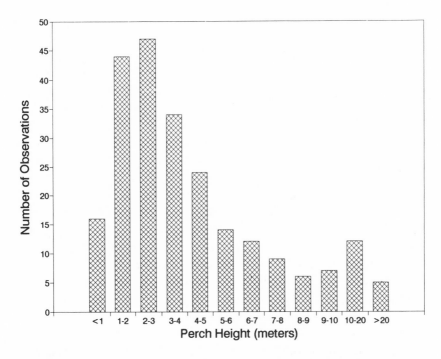

Figure 7. Frequency distribution of recorded perch heights for *Corallus hortulanus* in the West Indies. Modified from Henderson (1993a).

West Indies, 64.8% were at heights of 1–5 m above ground (Figure 7). The largest snakes tended to perch close to ground level in ambush postures, presumably awaiting mammalian prey (Henderson, 1993a). More limited observations of *C. hortulanus* in populations outside of the West Indies suggest similar foraging strategies and habitat use.

Corallus hortulanus is essentially arboreal in habits. However, the stomach of one museum specimen has been found to contain two terrestrial frogs (*Elachistocleis ovalis*), which suggests the snakes may occasionally descend to feed on the ground. Under captive conditions *C. hortulanus* has often been observed to capture prey on the floor of its cage, and then "carry" the dead animal in a coil up into the safety of the branches before swallowing it.

In its choice of food, the Common tree boa is the least specialized of the four species, preying on anurans, lizards (including small *Basiliscus basiliscus*, *Iguana iguana*, and various *Anolis*), birds (particularly small passerines), rats (principally the roof rat, *Rattus rattus*), mice, opossum, and other small mammals, including bats. *Corallus hortulanus* exhibits marked geographic differences in diet. Henderson (1993b) found that on the mainland (but including Trinidad and Tobago), 52 prey items included 3 lizards (1 *Basiliscus* and 2 unidentified), 17 birds (including flycatchers: Tyrannidae), and 32 mammals. The mammals included opossums and bats, but mostly murid rodents (*Akodon*, *Mus*, *Rattus*). Mass ratios (prey mass/snake mass) were determined for two of the birds: a snake 533 mm SVL had a mass ratio of 0.20 (i.e., the prey item had a mass 20% of the snake's mass), and a snake 496 mm SVL had a mass ratio of 0.44. Few prey records are available for snakes less than 500 mm SVL, but birds were taken by snakes as small as 431 mm SVL. Snakes 500–575 mm SVL ate birds and mammals with about equal frequency, but snakes 750–1630 mm SVL fed primarily on mammals (Figure 8). In contrast to mainland *C. hortulanus* where lizards comprise a rather insignificant proportion of the diet, lizards (almost exclusively *Anolis*) accounted for 67.2% of 64 prey items in West Indian tree boa populations (Figure 9; Henderson, 1993b). Conversely, birds are rarely taken by *Corallus* in the West Indies (4.7% of 64 records) (Figure 9), and although no bats have been recorded from stomach contents, recent observations by Henderson on Grenada strongly suggest that they are eaten. As on the mainland, *C. hortulanus* in the West Indies undergoes an ontogenetic shift in diet. However, whereas the shift is from birds and bats to rodents on the mainland, it is from lizards to rodents in the West Indies (Figure 10). Snakes less than 600 mm SVL prey exclusively on anoles, those 600–1100 mm SVL take anoles and endotherms (with the latter comprising a greater proportion of total prey with increasing SVL), and tree boas larger than 1100

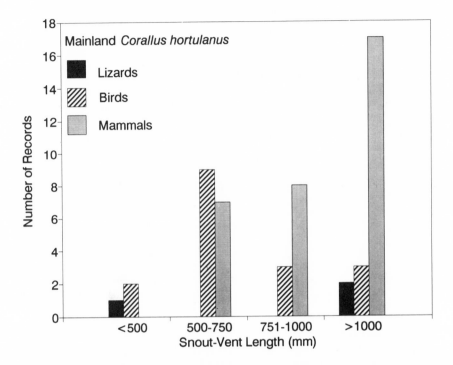

Figure 8. Frequency occurrence of lizards, birds, and mammals in the diet of four size classes of mainland *Corallus hortulanus* (based on 52 prey items). Modified from Henderson (1993b).

mm SVL prey exclusively on endotherms. Mean mass ratios for lizards was 0.094 (range: 0.009–0.296) whereas mean mass ratios for rodents was 0.159 (range: 0.067–0.286). The differences are not significantly different (Henderson, 1993a).

Wehekind (1974) gives a graphic account of a specimen in captivity which struck and captured a bat on the wing, and in parts of its range bats form an important element of its diet. *Corallus h. hortulanus* may be found living among small trees and shrubs at the edge of forest trails, where the snakes feed on the numerous species of bats that use the cleared openings as nocturnal flight paths. O'Shea (1990) describes one such trail in dry

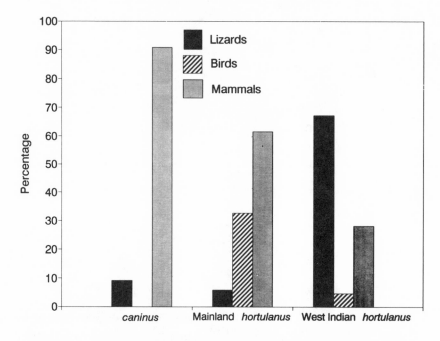

Figure 9. Frequency of occurrence of lizards, birds, and mammals in the diets of *Corallus caninus*, mainland populations of *C. hortulanus*, and West Indian populations of *C. hortulanus*. Modified from Henderson (1993b).

terra-firme forest on the riverine island of Maracá, Brazil, along which he found 11 *C. hortulanus* of five different color varieties, one of which had recently eaten a bat. The Cuban boa (*Epicrates angulifer*) and the Puerto Rican boa (*Epicrates inornatus*) have been noted to adopt a similar sit-and-wait foraging strategy, capturing bats on the wing as they emerge from the entrances of caves (Hardy, 1957; Rodríguez and Reagan, 1984). *Corallus hortulanus* has also been observed to habitually frequent bat-pollinated trees, striking at bats in flight as they feed from the nectar-bearing flowers, documented by Hopkins and Hopkins (1982). On Grenada, *C. hortulanus* inhabits drier areas and is said to be

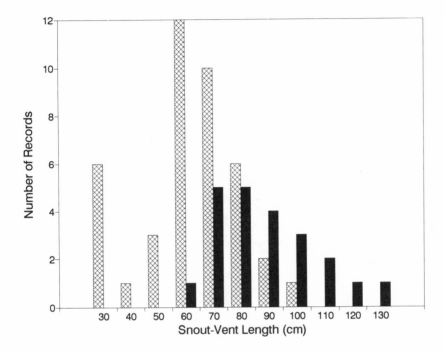

Figure 10. Frequency distribution of the incidence of lizard prey (cross-hatched bars) and endothermic prey (solid black bars) in the diet of various size classes of *Corallus hortulanus* in the West Indies (30 = 30–39.9 cm; 40 = 40–49.9 cm, etc.). Modified from Henderson (1993a).

an excellent "rat-catcher", occasionally entering the roofs of houses.

The Common tree boa has perfected a novel technique for climbing thin vertical tree trunks which have no side branches to facilitate leverage; the snake reaches upward and grips the trunk by coiling around it with the anterior part of its body. It then pulls the rest of the body up and uses the posterior half to re-anchor itself, enabling the snake to reach higher and move further upwards in the same way.

Figure 11. Distribution of *Corallus hortulanus*. *C. h. hortulanus* (1) and *C. h. cooki* (2).

THE EMERALD TREE BOA
(*Corallus caninus*)

This is the most massive and most brilliantly colored of the four species of tree boas. It is known under various other names, such as Dog boa, Yellow-faced boa, Parrot snake, together with numerous local names, including *Falsa mapanare verde* and *Boa esmeralda* (Venezuela), *Arara(m)bia, Cobra papagio, Cobra verde* (Amazonian Brazil), and *Yea-tah-yah-mo* (Akawai Indian, Guyana). The neonates of this boa are dramatically different in color to that of the adult snake, which has in the past resulted in the erroneous descriptions of new species. No subspecies are recognized. Within the genus, *C. caninus* would seem to have the closest phylogenetic affinities with *C. cropanii*, the least known species of all (Kluge, 1991). The Emerald tree boa is illustrated in Plates 34–38; a strikingly similar pythonine species, *Morelia viridis* (Green tree python), is shown on Plate 39.

Etymology

The specific name *caninus* is Latin, meaning "of dogs", which probably alludes to the doglike appearance of the head with its long anterior maxillary teeth.

41

Geographic Range

Corallus caninus is restricted to Amazonian and Guianan South America: Colombia, Venezuela, Ecuador, Peru, Bolivia, Brazil, Guyana, Suriname, and French Guiana. There is a questionable published record from west of the Andes (Niceforo-Maria, 1942). Altitudinal distribution is from sea level to about 1000 m. The distribution of *C. caninus* is largely coincident with the distribution of lowland tropical rain forest. It is absent from caatinga and Atlantic Rain Forest in eastern Brazil. *Corallus caninus* occurs only in areas that receive more than 1500 mm of precipitation annually.

Description

Maximum SVL is at least 1530 mm. The general habitus is that of a large, chunky head, long anterior maxillary teeth, slender neck, strongly laterally compressed body, and prehensile tail. The dorsal ground color in juveniles is yellow (rarely retained in adults) or brick-red or pinkish brown; in adults it is some shade of green. The transition from juvenile to adult coloration (based on wild-caught specimens) is gradual and normally occurs in snakes 550–600 mm SVL, although they may be as small as 450–500 mm SVL. The ventral ground color in juveniles is usually beige or dull yellow and usually immaculate. In adults, the ventral ground color is off-white, cream, or some shade of yellow (dull to bright); ventrals and subcaudals are usually immaculate, but may occasionally be flecked with some shade of green. The underside of the head is normally some shade of yellow, immaculate or flecked or washed with green (sometimes quite heavily). The labials are some shade of yellow and are frequently flecked or washed with green. The ventral ground color encroaches onto the dorsal scale rows, with more anterior than posterior scale rows affected. The encroaching yellow is usually flecked with green, sometimes heavily. Enamel white markings are customarily present on the lateral and dorsal surfaces. The dorsal-most markings are usually triangular in shape, with the base of the triangle on the dorsal midline; the triangles may be connected by a middorsal line or not connected. The triangles are often absent anteriorly (resulting in no anterior pattern or just a middorsal stripe, either continuous or broken), becoming prominent and elongate (to the point of losing their triangular shape and appearing as white lines perpendicular to the dorsal mid-line) at midbody; posteriorly, they are shorter and broader. Frequently the dorsal ground color surrounding the triangles is heavily stippled with dark green to black in adults, and brown in yellowish phase juveniles. Lateral blotches may be absent or greatly reduced anteriorly, becoming more prominent at midbody and posteriorly. There is considerable geographic variation in the extent of the lateral white blotches: snakes from eastern Venezuela, Guyana, Suriname, and northeastern Brazil (Roraima) frequently lack lateral markings or have them much reduced; snakes from western Brazil (Rondônia, Mato Grosso) also lack lateral white markings. In extreme cases (snakes from Guyana), the dorsum is devoid of any white markings. In contrast, snakes from Amazonia (exceptions noted) have conspicuous lateral white blotches, and they are especially pronounced in snakes from the easternmost region of Amazonia (Maranhao) and the upper Amazon of Ecuador and Peru, but there are frequent exceptions. In extreme cases, the normally dorsoventrally oriented elongate blotches (1–2 scales wide $\times$ 4–10 scales long) are almost round and may be 4 $\times$ 4 scales in dimension.

There is virtually no sexual dimorphism in traditional meristic characters. Ranges are as follows: dorsal scale rows at midbody 61–84; ventrals 186–218; subcaudals 62–84; ventrals + subcaudals 256–285; supralabials (with deep labial pits) 9–13; infralabials (with deep labial pits) 11–16; scales between supraorbitals 4–15; loreals 2–5; subloreals 2–10; loreals + subloreals 2–14; circumorbital scales 9–19; nasals usually in contact, with 3–12 scales bordering nasals (Figure 12).

The hemipenis (based on a specimen from Brazil) is shallowly forked, extending to the 9th subcaudal, the organ dividing at the 7th subcaudal and the sulcus dividing at the 6th subcaudal.

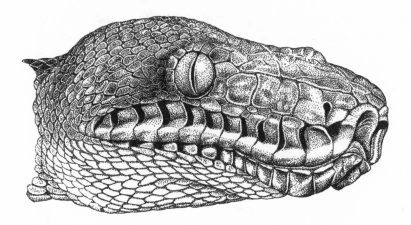

Figure 12. Head detail of *Corallus caninus*, illustrating the well-developed heat-sensitive labial pits. Drawing by Peter J. Stafford.

The basal one-third is nude with prominent sulcal folds. Distally, there are six flounces that fuse with the sulcal folds and are most prominent on the sulcal surface; the flounces occur before the bifurcation. The most proximal flounce is reduced in size and extended into a small papilla on the asulcate surface. The sulcal folds extend to the tips of the short arms which bear only a few papillate flounces (Branch, 1981).

Longevity

Corallus caninus appears to be relatively long-lived. A wild-caught adult female in the collection of the St. Louis Zoo lived in captivity for 15 years, 5 months and 27 days (Bowler, 1977).

Ecological Data

One of the most striking features of this snake is its extraordinary resemblance to the Green tree python (*Morelia* [=*Chondropython*] *viridis*) of Papua New Guinea and northern Australia. These two distantly related species have evolved convergently as an adaptive response to their similar environment and way of life. They share virtually the same coloration and neonate ontogenetic color change sequence, and have the same unique way of coiling the body into symmetrical loops over a horizontal branch while at rest. The bright green coloration broken with white provides excellent camouflage among the leaves and dappled sunlight up in the branches, and similarly, the juvenile brownish color may serve to disguise young snakes in the more poorly lit understory vegetation. Both brown and yellow-colored juveniles may also actively seek out darkened resting sites for the purposes of concealment, as observed with the convergent *Morelia viridis* (Garrett and Smith, 1994).

Corallus caninus occurs most commonly in wet lowland rain forest, living among the canopy foliage of trees and shrubs, particularly over water (Figure 13). It occurs in areas that receive in excess of 1500 mm of rain annually. Chippaux (1986) gives its altitudinal range in French Guiana as between sea level and approximately 100 meters, although Pérez-Santos and Moreno (1988) cite an example from Colombia seen at an elevation of 824 meters. It is found in both primary and secondary vegetation, and also occurs in swamp forest. Duellman (1978) described finding an adult specimen coiled on the ground in direct sunlight, although as a rule the species is nocturnal and rarely descends from the branches. During the day it remains inactive, looped over a horizontal branch in an ellipsoidal coil with its head in the center. When coiled "asleep" in this way the snake may also tuck its head between its coils. Captive specimens will sometimes behave in the same way when "sprinkled" with water for the purposes of increasing humidity in the vivarium. Emerald tree boas are most usually found active between approximately 1700 hours to 0500 hours.

Diet

The species shows a strong preference for endothermic prey (Figure 9). Of 11 prey items recovered by Henderson (1993b), 10 were mammals, most were murid rodents, including two

Figure 13.   Distribution of *Corallus caninus*.

Oecomys bicolor; one *O. bicolor* had a volume of 17 cm³ in a
snake 430 mm SVL. Mammals were taken by snakes 430–1451
mm SVL. One snake, 380 mm SVL and the smallest snake
from which a prey item was recovered, contained a gekkonid
lizard (tentatively identified as *Thecadactylus rapicauda*).

Schulte (1988) calculated a population density of one *Corallus
caninus* per 2.7 km², but felt that the estimate was questionable
due to the lack of more precise data regarding movement ecology. Schulte also felt that *C. caninus* was persecuted because of its
resemblance to the pit-viper *Bothriopsis bilineata*, a species that is
widely sympatric with *C. caninus* over much of its range and
which has the potential of delivering a lethal bite to humans.

In captivity *Corallus caninus* will forage for food in much the same way as has been observed in *C. hortulanus*, moving slowly through the branches and periodically lowering and raising its head to investigate adjacent branches.

Emerald tree boas are generally regarded as rather irascible and aggressive snakes. Specimens collected in the wild have been described as making no effort to escape until seized, whereupon they strike viciously and apply their powers of constriction with full force (Beebe, 1946). However, after a preliminary struggle they relax and seem to accept captivity with a sort of "watchful waiting".

Agonistic behavior between males housed together in captivity with a female has also been observed in this species. Osborne (1984) described aggression between two males, which included chasing, mounting, and writhing body movements until one male finally became dominant. This snake would then continue to pursue the subordinate male and attempt to overpower it, using the posterior part of the body to constrict the neck area, and not the anterior part normally used in constricting prey. This behavior was only observed when the two snakes were coiled on the same, or nearby horizontal branches: no biting was involved. On occasion the dominant male was also observed to "attack" and constrict the female.

THE ANNULATED TREE BOA
(*Corallus annulatus*)

Only in recent years has any information on the habits and reproductive biology of this species, also known as the Ringed tree
boa and Brown dog-headed boa, been forthcoming. Three subspecies have been described: *C. a. annulatus*, *C. a. blombergi*, and
C. a. colombianus, although the distinction between them is based
largely on small and insubstantial differences in scalation. The
validity of *C. a. blombergi*, and particularly *C. a. colombianus*, has
been questioned (Peters, 1957; Henderson, 1993c), while differences in the jaw bones of some *C. annulatus* specimens from
Colombia and Ecuador suggests the existence of an undescribed
species of tree boa (Kluge, 1991). The Annulated tree boa is
illustrated in Plates 40–46.

Etymology

The specific name *annulatus* is from the Latin meaning "ringed",
a probable reference to the ringlike markings on the dorsum; the
subspecific name *blombergi* is a patronym given in honor of the

49

explorer Rolf Blomberg, while *colombianus* refers to the country of Colombia.

Geographic Range

Corallus annulatus occurs from northern Honduras to southern Ecuador west of the Andes. Its known distribution is disjunct, with large hiatuses occurring between northern Honduras and southeastern Nicaragua, and between western Colombia (area of the Río San Juan) and western Ecuador. Altitudinal distribution is from at or near sea level to at least 300–400 m above sea level. Henderson (1993c) questioned the locality data of the holotype. Although other specimens of *C. annulatus* have been collected in Ecuador, the holotype of *C. a. blombergi* is the only specimen from Ecuador recorded from east of the Andes (Rendahl and Vestergren, 1941). The collector of *C. a. blombergi* did have specimens from the Guayaquil area (west of the Andes) in the collection along with material from eastern Ecuador, and *C. annulatus* is known from that area (Figure 14).

Description

Maximum SVL is at least 1335 mm (Panama). The general habitus is that of a large chunky head, long anterior maxillary teeth, labials with deep pits, a slender neck, a strongly prehensile tail, and a laterally compressed body. The dorsal ground color occurs in variable shades of brown, but predominantly red-brown (or occasionally taupe to khaki) in Central America and northern Colombia, to milk chocolate- or dark chocolate-brown. Snakes from southern Central America undergo an ontogenetic color change from vivid brick-red or burnt orange to more subdued shades of brown; it is currently unknown whether or not snakes from Ecuador undergo an ontogenetic change in dorsal coloration. The primary element in the dorsal pattern is a fairly well-defined rhomboid marking anteriorly that deteriorates

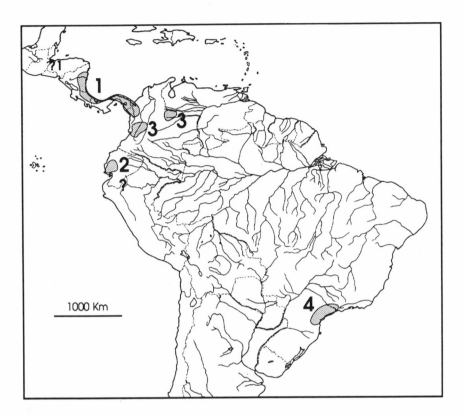

Figure 14. Distribution of *Corallus annulatus annulatus* (1), *C. a. blombergi* (2), *C. a. colombianus* (3), and *Corallus cropanii* (4).

anteroposteriorly, at midbody having a rhomboidlike shape with rounded edges, frequently larger on the top half than on the bottom half, or sometimes ovoid at midbody. Posteriorly, the shapes once again become more diamondlike, but not as well defined as immediately posterior to the head. The main elements of the dorsal pattern may be conjoined at or near the dorsal midline. The central area of the dorsal elements are colored similarly to the dorsal ground color in Central American and Colombian snakes and may include a small whitish blotch in the ventral-most portion of the element; in material from Ecuador, the central blotch area is conspicuously paler than the dorsal ground color. There are 36–46 dorsal body blotches that, at midbody, are 8–13 scales wide in Central American snakes and 6–9 scales wide in specimens from Ecuador. Stripes on the head are variable in definition and number as follows: 2 postorbital stripes + 1 central stripe on the top of the head, 2 postorbital stripes, 1 postorbital stripe + one central stripe on the top of the head, or 1 postorbital stripe. The stripes may be solid and well defined, broken up, or comprised of fine stippling and faint relative to the ground color. The underside of the head is usually lightly stippled along the infralabials and gulars, occasionally immaculate, or rarely heavily stippled on infralabials and gulars; stippling is usually absent from the central gulars around the mental groove. The ventral ground color is extremely variable, being white, pale dull yellow, yellow-tan, pale beige, pale copper, pale red-brown, or taupe. The pattern on the venter is some shade of brown (frequently taupe) and usually consists of dots, flecks, and smudges, sometimes occurring on the entire ventral surface of the body, or restricted to the posterior portion of the body. Subcaudals always have some flecks or smudges in some shade of brown (frequently taupe).

The available sample size is inadequate to determine if any scale characters are sexually dimorphic. Dorsal scales at midbody are in 50–57 rows. Ventrals are 251–269 and subcaudals are 76–88. Supralabials are 12–14; infralabials are 15–18; and scales between supraorbitals are 7–10. There are usually 3 (rarely 4) loreals; supraloreals are 3–5; infraloreals are 2–7; loreals+infraloreals are 6–12; circumorbital scales are 12–16; and the nasals are usually not in contact.

Longevity

The Philadelphia Zoo gives a record of an adult (sex unknown) wild-caught *C. annulatus* having lived for 12 years, 4 months and 4 days in captivity (Bowler, 1977).

Ecological Data

Corallus annulatus occurs at elevations below 400 meters, mostly in primary and secondary rain forest vegetation. Through its occasional discovery in consignments of tropical fruits, it would also appear to inhabit plantain and banana groves, and perhaps other fruit plantations.

From most reports *C. annulatus* would seem to be a rare and seldom seen snake throughout its range. There is little information available on its habits and behavior in nature, although a number of observations have been made of the species in zoological collections. Most success in breeding *C. annulatus* has been in the United States, where a number of adult snakes from Costa Rica have for some years been maintained at Houston, Fort Worth, and San Diego zoos. Captive observations have shown that it is behaviorally the most divergent species of the genus, and in many ways would seem to be more similar to the Malagasy *Sanzinia madagascariensis* than its generic relatives. In particular, and unlike *C. hortulanus* and *C. caninus*, the species has a relatively mild disposition. It has a tendency to secrete itself tightly between cage furnishings in much the same way as has been observed in *Sanzinia*, and it is less inclined to perch exposed up in the branches, preferring to shelter under roots, buttresses, in tree hollows and in epiphytic growth in its natural environment. In captivity it has been shown to favor terrestrial refuge sites or an elevated hidebox lined with Sphagnum moss. In its choice of prey, captive adult specimens have shown a preference for rodents and birds. In the wild it is known to prey on small rodents (Henderson et al., 1995).

CROPANI'S BOA
(*Corallus cropanii*)

This rare and unusual snake is only known from the original description published by A. R. Hoge in 1954 (Figure 15). It is represented by perhaps no more than three specimens in museum collections. The species is distinguished, not only from other species of *Corallus*, but from all other boas by having a low number of relatively large dorsal scales.

Etymology

The name *cropanii* is a patronym given in honor of Ottorino de Fiori, Baron de Cropani, Director of the Instituto Vulcanológico at Catania, Brazil.

Geographic Range

Corallus cropanii is only known from the vicinity of the type locality, Miracatu, in the state of São Paulo, Brazil. The total known range is only about 600 km².

Figure 15. *Corallus cropanii*. Drawing by Peter J. Stafford (based on a photograph by A. R. Hoge).

Description

Cropani's boa attains a SVL of at least 1.4 meters. It has a somewhat stouter, less laterally compressed body compared to other *Corallus*, and a prehensile tail that is also rather short (14–18% of body length in males). The dorsum is olive green to beige, patterned with 36–38 pale, copper to dark brown diamond-shaped markings that continue on to the tail, and a series of smaller blotches placed laterally. The venter is white to dull yellow, with the lateral edges and subcaudals marked with dark brown.

The hemipenis is weakly bilobed (organ to subcaudal 7, bilobed at 7); the most proximal flounce is at subcaudal 3, the flounces grading into large calyces with scalloped edges distally. Coarse papillae are set at the apex and the sulcus spermaticus is forked.

Supralabials 10–14, with well-developed labial pits; infralabials 14, with well-developed labial pits; loreals 2; scales around eye 9–10; nasals not in contact, with 3 adjacent scales; dorsal scales in 29–32 rows at midbody; ventrals 179–200; subcaudals 51–53.

Ecological Data

Corallus cropanii is arguably the rarest boid in the world, but it is unquestionably the rarest boid in the New World. Virtually nothing is known about the natural history of this snake, other than it occurs on or near the coastal plain in the vicinity of Miracatu, State of São Paulo, at an elevation of 40–45 meters above sea level. Presumably *C. cropanii* at one time had a more extensive range in the Atlantic Rain Forests of Brazil. The three localities from which this species has been taken all occur within a narrow strip of degraded forest, and all are within 50–100 km of São Paulo, a megalopolis with a population of about 16 million inhabitants, regarded as the third largest city in the world, and possibly the fastest growing city in the world. The Atlantic Rain Forest was estimated to have at one time covered 1.0–1.5 million km^2, but 90–98% has been eliminated or severely degraded (summarized by Por, 1992). Although, as of 1991, São Paulo state has the largest nucleus of Atlantic Rain Forest, about 90% has been destroyed since the settlement of Brazil by Europeans (Victor, 1975; Por, 1992). Most of the clearing is attributable to shifting agriculture (i.e., using plots of land for 3–15 years and then clearing more land; Por, 1992). Based on the available locality data, Henderson et al. (1995) estimated the range of *C. cropanii* to be about 600 km^2; i.e., less than 0.02 the size of the next most geographically restricted tree boa (*C. annulatus*) and smaller than 0.0001 the size of the five geographically widespread boines (Henderson, 1994). The known range of *C. cropanii* is less than 1° of latitude. The amount of suitable habitat within the range is, however, undoubtedly much less than 600 km².

As far as is known, the species has never been maintained in captivity. Its proportionally thicker body and shorter tail suggest that it may be more of a ground-dwelling snake, or at least not so well adapted to an arboreal existence as the other species of *Corallus*.

CAPTIVE HUSBANDRY AND BREEDING

Information on the successful maintenance and breeding of tree boas has in recent times become much more widely available, and a great deal more is now known of their basic requirements in the vivarium. One of the earliest documented reports of these snakes in captivity was published in 1893 by A. E. Brown, who described the scalation and colors of several *Corallus hortulanus* and *C. annulatus* held at the time in the collection of the Philadelphia Zoo. Keeping exotic reptiles for zoological exhibition was at this time, however, still very much in its infancy. In many cases it was not known how the animals should be properly maintained in an artificial environment, or protected from disease, and more often than not they did not survive very long. Captive-raised tree boas and aspects of their herpetoculture are illustrated in Plates 47–53.

It is only in the last 30 years or so that major progress has been made in animal husbandry techniques and new medications developed for reptile diseases and ailments. During this time the interest in keeping snakes has grown tremendously, with substantial numbers of animals continuing to be taken from the wild. Precisely how many are captured each year for the pet trade is difficult to put a figure on, though between 1977 and 1983 it is known that more than four thousand *Corallus hortulanus* were imported into the United States alone (Dodd, 1986). During the same 7-year period a total of 550 *C. caninus* and three *C. annulatus* were imported. To some extent this reflects the greater rarity of *caninus* and *annulatus*, although all tree boas are subject to the same level of threat and are listed by CITES (1973), the Convention on International Trade in Endangered Species of Wild Fauna and Flora. All *Corallus* (including *Xenoboa*) are defined as "not necessarily now threatened with extinction but may become so unless trade is strictly regulated" (IUCN, 1979). We cannot stress enough the need for those persons interested in maintaining tree boas in captivity to seek out captive-bred animals rather than wild-caught individuals. *Corallus caninus*, and especially *C. hortulanus*, are bred fairly routinely in captivity and newborn snakes are available in numbers every year. Tree boas in the wild are faced with enough problems for survival (e.g., habitat destruction, introduced predators, persecution by humans) that commercial exploitation should not be added to the list of obstacles for survival. Captive propagation is now fulfilling the demand for these interesting snakes, and the techniques involved are well documented (see literature sections).

The Right Living Conditions

The behavior and natural habitat of tree boas requires that they be maintained under a certain set of environmental conditions, i.e., warm, humid, tropical conditions, with a period of daylight and darkness and ample opportunities for climbing. In large-scale zoological collections with the resources for exhibiting reptiles in spacious accommodations, snakes are usually displayed in large enclosures attractively decorated with living plants, pieces of tree stump and natural-looking rockwork, more for the benefit of the visiting public than the occupants. The size of the enclosure, within reason, would not seem to be particularly important, however. In private facilities where space may be limited, the snakes can be accommodated equally well in glass aquaria. Particularly suitable are large glass vivaria made to measure with sliding glass or plexiglass panels at the front for access and taller in their dimensions than wide or deep to provide for the snake's habit of climbing upwards. Glass has the added benefit of being easy to clean, and also holds humidity better than cages made, for example, of wood, but melamine-faced chipboard is a good and also lighter alternative. There has recently become available a range of commercially constructed vivaria that are equally suitable for housing tree boas. Whatever the size, dimensions, and construction of the vivarium, it is important that it be well ventilated and allow for the free circulation of air.

Vivarium Furnishings

The interior of the tree boa vivarium should be well furnished with stout branches for the snakes to climb. These are best affixed to the side, or arranged in such a way that the floor can be cleaned without having to remove them and disturb the occupants unnecessarily. In conditions of good light, robust foliage plants such as aroids (*Monstera* spp. and *Philodendron* spp.), small woody-stemmed trees (i.e. *Ficus benjamina, F. lyrata*), cane-cut false palms (*Yucca* spp. and *Dracaena* spp.), and bromeliads of various kinds can be included for effect and to provide additional climbing opportunities. Artificial plants can also be used to good effect in enhancing the appearance of the vivarium interior. The floor may be left bare or covered with damp Sphagnum moss, bark chips, leaves, or more hygienically, with absorbent paper (e.g., newspaper). Wood shavings can also be used as a ground medium, but these have sometimes been known to become lodged in a snake's mouth when feeding, causing lacerations of the interior lining and leading to disease.

Corallus hortulanus thrives under fairly dry conditions in captivity, but for *C. caninus* and *C. annulatus* humidity is more important and should be maintained at a higher level between approximately 75% and 85%. Some keepers of *C. caninus* have found that this species responds better to captive conditions if sprinkled regularly with water, or even kept over water to provide high humidity. The snakes may also prefer to drink from the droplets of water that collect on their coils rather than drink from a dish. It does not seem necessary for a large container of water to be available in which the snake can completely submerge, as unlike some other boids it is not in the nature of tree boas to habitually immerse themselves for long periods. However, a small vessel of water from which to drink should always be provided.

Tree boas often prefer to coil among the branches of their vivarium during the day, but it is also recommended that an elevated hidebox or similar refuge be made available, especially for *C. annulatus*. A hollowed-out log can be used for this and fixed securely in the fork of a branch. Alternatively, an equally suitable, if less natural-looking hidebox can be constructed from plywood, with a hole in one side through which the snake can enter, and a removable lid for ease of cleaning. This can be lined with a "nest" of dry sphagnum moss or absorbent paper, both of which are easy to change when soiled.

Temperature and Lighting

The temperature in the vivarium must be maintained between 26 °C and 32 °C during the day and not allowed to fall below 22 °C for any length of time at night. If using small cage units there are various electrical heaters available by which this can be achieved. Electrical fan heaters tend to produce a very dry atmosphere and are not recommended. As animals which habitually climb up to the top of their enclosure and perch on the highest branches, the best means of heating is from above by way of a ceramic heat lamp, spot lamp, or similar thermostatically controlled element. If placed in the center of the vivarium so that heat is reflected downwards, the snakes will choose for themselves a position where they find the temperature most comfortable.

As snakes, which for the most part are active only by night, the provision of direct natural sunlight does not seem to be necessary for their well-being and successful husbandry. Some illumination, however, should be provided during the day. A fluorescent tube, an incandescent light bulb, or spot lamp is generally all that is needed and will suit the purpose adequately. The lights should be left on for approximately 11 to 12 hours each day, which corresponds to the normal ratio of day length and darkness in the tropics.

Health

It is important that tree boas, like all other snakes, are kept in a hygienic environment. A large enclosure decorated with living plants and natural materials may be more interesting to look at but is also more difficult to keep clean, and in the case of tree boas, the risk of disease may be further increased by the warm, humid living conditions which these particular snakes favor. This has convinced many herpetoculturists that these animals are best kept in small cage units under artificial, almost sterile conditions, so that their environment can be more easily controlled. This is certainly more practical, especially when the snakes themselves may be indifferent to the nature of the materials around them. Overall it is probably true to say that most snake keepers find an arrangement somewhere in between the most acceptable solution.

Whatever opinions the individual may have on how best to maintain tree boas and other snakes in captivity, it is good husbandry practice to keep any newly acquired animals segregated from established stock and give them a quarantine period of at least a month. This not only allows the keeper to more easily watch for signs of contagious diseases, which might otherwise put other snakes at serious risk, but provides the new snake with time to "settle in" to the vivarium environment.

Shedding Problems

A common problem from which tree boas suffer in captivity is difficulty with shedding their skin, or "sloughing" as it is more correctly known. The old skin layer (epidermis) sometimes dries hard onto the new layer beneath, especially in the region of the neck and upper body, and the snake is unable to discard it in the usual way. These partial moults are often indicative of dehydration, caused by insufficient water intake or atmospheric humidity, but may also be a result of infrequent or underfeeding and ill-health. In serious cases this remaining dead skin can be very difficult to remove but every attempt should be made to get rid of it, especially the pieces covering the eyes, so as to avoid the ever-present risk of infection. To remove this skin, the snake should be immersed in a container of warm water, leaving sufficient room, of course, for it to keep its head above the water level. After a few hours of soaking, any remaining skin can usually be peeled away fairly easily. Alternatively, the snake can be placed in a wet cloth bag, containing some wet cardboard, sphagnum moss, or similar absorbent material, which the animal can use to rub itself against to help loosen the skin. It is important that the snake always be given sufficient time to slough in the natural way and the skin not removed prematurely, as this would almost certainly lead to widespread infection and possibly death. Physical injuries to the skin itself, such as superficial cuts, wounds, and torn-off scales, can be treated with an iodine-based antiseptic such as Pevadine, or a very dilute solution (5%) of hydrogen peroxide, and kept dry.

Skin Infections

The consequences of not taking sufficient care to provide clean, hygienic living conditions can be disastrous and the cause of prolonged, unnecessary suffering. Under warm and humid conditions fungi and bacteria flourish, and in a particularly wet, insanitary environment, infections of the skin are all the more difficult to avoid, often leading to disease. One of the most common forms of disease is caused by the bacteria *Pseudomonas* or *Aeromonas*, which in serious cases leads to necrosis of the affected areas of skin and sometimes death. Medical treatment is normally required for bacterial infections of this kind, usually with an antibiotic drug to which the particular strain of bacteria responsible is sensitive and has no natural resistance. While usually an effective cure however, it would be unwise of the inexperienced snake keeper to use such drugs without the direction of a qualified professional who can advise on the correct number of dosages, length of treatment, and possible side affects.

The *Pseudomonas* bacterium is often also the cause of ulcerative stomatitis, a similar disease of the mouth characterized by small cheesy deposits and necrosis of the gums, and also of infections of the upper intestinal tract. The drug Gentamycin, given at the rate of 2.5 mg/kg body weight as an intramuscular injection, has proved to be one of the most effective cures for these diseases, but it can cause dehydration and should be administered together with subcutaneous injections of saline to compensate for loss of fluids and electrolytes. Chloromycetin has also been used to good effect, and this can be administered more easily with oral dosages of 50 mg/kg body weight.

Respiratory Disorders

Respiratory disorders are another form of infection that may require treatment with antibiotics. In particular, it is not uncommon for tree boas to suffer from breathing difficulties and congestion of the nasal passages, usually caused by the snakes being kept at too low a temperature. Distressed animals invariably begin to hold their mouth agape when the nostrils and airways become choked, and the throat may also appear distended. In some cases, it may be sufficient to increase the temperature in the cage to about 33 °C for a week or so, but for more serious infections, including pneumonia, antibiotics should be considered, using Terramycin (50 mg/kg body weight), Chloromycetin

(30 mg/kg body weight), or Streptomycin (50 mg/kg body weight), according to veterinary instruction.

Internal Parasites

Tree boas are commonly afflicted by internal parasites, such as worms of various kinds, but these do not normally constitute a serious threat to their well-being. Under captive conditions however, they can become more of a health problem. Nematode worms are frequently found in snakes imported from the wild. These parasites normally reside in the intestinal tract where they can be eradicated using dog or cat worming tablets with a base of piperazine citrate dissolved in water and given orally at the rate of 5 mg/100 g of body weight. As part of their life-cycle, however, they migrate to other parts of the body to encyst, and so the treatment should be repeated periodically to kill any that may escape the initial dose. Similarly, tapeworms in the gut can be removed with Yomesan, a commercial preparation, using a dosage of 150 mg/kg body weight. These worms can grow quite large and there is a reliable record of a worm measuring 3 meters being removed from a large anaconda. Tapeworm infestation is more usually diagnosed by finding the individual segments of the worms in the feces of infected snakes.

Gastroenteritis

A more dangerous disease, which tree boas are prone to suffer from, is gastroenteritis, caused by the protozoan, *Entamoeba invadens*. Snakes imported from the wild and not maintained under proper hygiene conditions in transit are particularly prone to this disease. Symptoms include a loss of appetite, regurgitation of food, and pale, slimy stools accompanied by excessive fluid. The Emerald tree boa would seem to be particularly sensitive to the effects of this disease, which, if not treated, develops rapidly and is likely to be fatal. Providing it is diagnosed at an early stage however, and before any damage to the intestinal wall has occurred, it can normally be quickly and effectively cured with the drugs Flagyl (250 mg/kg body weight), and Emtryl (150 mg/kg body weight), used for treating the condition in domestic animals and humans.

Ticks and Mites

External parasites in the form of ticks and mites are more easily eradicated. Ticks are most often found on the skin and beneath the scales of snakes captured in the wild. They are fairly easily removed by first dabbing them with 100% alcohol, and, after they relinquish their hold, gently extracting them, taking care not to leave the mouthparts behind which may otherwise cause local infection. Mites, on the other hand, can prove more of a problem. Within a short space of time these tiny black parasites can reach plague proportions, often congregating around the eyes; very heavy infestations are characterized by the snake's body becoming covered by their white, powdery droppings. An infected snake should be kept in a well-ventilated vivarium with a small piece of a dichlorvos-impregnated insecticide strip, which should be left in place for as long as it takes to kill all the mites, usually 2 or 3 days. It may be necessary to repeat the treatment a week or so later to eliminate any others that may have emerged afterwards from eggs and escaped exposure to the insecticide.

Food and Feeding

Tree boas will normally accept most kinds of small animals as food in captivity. Their individual tastes, however, may vary considerably, and it is not uncommon for a snake to develop a liking for one kind of prey and, after a while, refuse all others. Certain snakes, for example, will only eat white mice and reject all other kinds of food, including mice of any other color. Similarly, some snakes will eat as many animals as they can manage at one meal, while others will only ever accept a single prey item.

For these reasons it is a good idea, if possible, to try and vary the diet. This may also help to stimulate the snake's appetite.

Small mammals and birds are, in most cases, the most easily obtainable food items, and they provide all the nutritional requirements a snake needs from a meal. Small lizards, such as *Anolis* spp. and geckos, may also be accepted, but unless the keeper is prepared to take the trouble of maintaining a breeding colony to provide a constant supply, it is generally an impractical food source to rely on. Care should be taken not to overfeed snakes, as this has been shown to be detrimental to their health and reproductive vigor. As a guide, an adult tree boa can be maintained perfectly well on a meal of two mice every 10 days or so, though young snakes are best fed more frequently, and neonates should be fed every 3 to 4 days. A good indication of when a snake is hungry is when it begins to start moving around its vivarium at an earlier time each evening and for longer periods.

Prey animals should be offered to the snake dead. Some snakes will quite readily accept food from the floor of their vivarium, but in other cases it may be offered on the end of long forceps or a stick. An established captive tree boa may accept food at any time of the day and show little concern if disturbed while eating, but young and wild-caught snakes usually require more patience and may take quite some time before starting to feed of their own accord.

Should an individual not accept food at all, it is usually because it is either being kept in an unsuitable environment or is ill. For the snake to feel at ease in captivity it must be provided with the proper living conditions, and may steadfastly refuse to feed if these are not absolutely right. In particular, tree boas will not feel secure unless they are provided with a small box to escape into, or some branches to wind themselves around and hide behind. In some cases only then, and after several days of uninterrupted solitude, will they begin to feed; it may help to screen the animal's vivarium to minimize disturbance. Tree boas often prefer to feed in the subdued light of evening or early morning or at night in total darkness, and certain individuals will only feed at these times. If the reason a snake does not feed is suspected to be due to ill health, the steps to be taken are fairly clear. In some cases, however, it might not be immediately obvious that a snake is ill, in which case it is worth arranging for a veterinary laboratory service to have a small quantity of the animal's fecal matter analyzed; this may reveal the presence of parasites, high levels of bacteria, or other internal abnormalities. There are other circumstances under which snakes will not feed. For example, it is usual and perfectly normal for them to hide away and stop feeding just before shedding their skin. Female snakes often stop feeding in the later stages of pregnancy, and some species naturally undergo a period of fasting at certain times of the year.

Breeding and Care of Young

By ensuring that the snakes are maintained under the right conditions, and providing that they are healthy and not unnecessarily disturbed, it should be possible, with a little patience, to breed them. The more commonly kept *Corallus hortulanus* has reproduced regularly in captivity (see literature sections), and would seem to be an easier snake to breed than any of its three relatives (there is no known record of *C. cropanii* in captivity). *Corallus caninus* was first bred in Europe at the Aquarium of Berlin Zoo in 1930, and for the second time a few years later at the Frankfurt Zoo (Meyer-Holzapfel, 1969), while *C. annulatus* does not seem to have reproduced in captivity until the mid-1970s. Results of successful breedings, especially of the Common tree boa, now frequently appear in herpetological publications, and even the rare Annulated tree boa has recently become better known following observations on its behavior and reproduction at the Dallas and Fort Worth Zoos (Murphy et al., 1978; Hudson, 1983; Blody and Mehaffey, 1989).

The most effective way of trying to breed tree boas is by maintaining a number of animals of the same taxon (species or subspecies) together in a breeding group, thereby increasing the chances of securing a compatible pair. This is, however, not always practical. The high purchase price and inherent management problems of keeping, for example, the Emerald tree boa, normally makes such an investment prohibitive to all but the most dedicated and enthusiastic of snake keepers. This also applies to the rarer Annulated tree boa, of which there are presently only a few breeding groups held in collections in the United States. The most widely available and easily kept of the four species of tree boas is the Common tree boa; consequently, more is known of how to keep and breed this species in captivity than any of its congeners. Although less "eye-catching" than the larger and brilliantly-colored *Corallus caninus*, the Common tree boa remains a popular exhibit in zoological vivaria and continues to be a favorite with private collectors. The more attractive red, yellow and orange forms in particular are highly prized and have become much sought after by specialist herpetoculturists interested in selectively breeding the species for color.

Mating behavior in captive tree boas usually takes place between December and March. At this time of year a drop in temperature of 3 °C to 4 °C and rise in humidity, simulating a change in the climate, often induces reproductive activity, particularly if the sexes have previously been maintained apart. Snakes that are kept alone for a period of time in this way often show an increased eagerness to mate when reintroduced to each other, and by housing the female together with more than one male, natural competition may also act as a stimulus and provide a further incentive for the dominant male to copulate. The temperature should be allowed to fall by turning the heat source off for a few hours in the evening, and by misting the snakes and the interior of the breeding cage heavily with water, the humidity will be increased measurably as well. Some also advocate spraying the snakes with cool water, preferably in the morning (Laszlo, 1983).

Tree boas usually mate during darkness or in the subdued light of evening and early morning and may remain coupled for several hours. It may be an energetic activity, with the male pursuing the female in courtship until she consents to mate, or the two snakes may simply lie coiled together among the branches with their tails entwined and cloacas coupled. Once copulation has started, there is usually little movement.

Development of the young is temperature-dependent and may take up to 250 days. During this time a spot lamp or other source of direct heat is recommended to provide the female with the opportunity to bask and "incubate" her developing brood. Walsh (1994) has monitored the position of gravid females in relation to four temperature zones. The results indicated that the snakes preferred temperatures that averaged 31 °C for most of the gestation period, but for the last few weeks prior to parturition they were observed to seek out cooler regions averaging 28 °C. Failure to provide an adequate thermal gradient, or keeping the snakes at too low or high an ambient temperature during the latter stages of pregnancy, may result in deformed and/or stillborn neonates. In the later stages of gestation, the female may only accept food sporadically or, more often, stop feeding altogether, but it is likely she will want to take regular drinks so a bowl of water should always be made available.

Depending on the time of copulation, birth can be expected to occur between the months of July and October. Some days before she is due to give birth the female will normally slough her skin. When birth becomes imminent she becomes very restless and descends to the ground in search of a secluded hiding place to crawl into. At this time a hidebox or similar refuge, lined with paper towel or damp Sphagnum moss, should be made available. For reasons somewhat obscure, females of C. caninus will sometimes give birth in the highest branches of their enclosure; to avoid possible injury to the neonates in such an event, the floor of the cage is best covered with a layer of moss or other soft material to cushion their fall. Alternatively, the female can be removed and maintained temporarily in smaller living quarters until parturition takes place. After giving birth the female usually begins to feed normally again within a few days, and again sloughs her skin. The size of the litter varies according to species and the size of the female; C. hortulanus: 2-(7)-12; C. caninus: 1-(10)-18; C. annulatus: 8-(11)-15 (minimum sample number of five with averages in parenthesis).

Rearing Baby Tree Boas

Neonates are best maintained separately in small plastic or glass containers, each furnished with a branch and water dish where the baby snakes can be given individual attention and their progress more easily monitored. They should be disturbed as little as possible and great care taken not to stress them unnecessarily, which might adversely affect their willingness to feed. The neonates may deteriorate quite quickly if they do not feed within a short time of birth and at regular intervals thereafter; however, because of the larger size of newborn C. *caninus* and their very slow metabolism, Walsh (1994) indicates that food need not be offered to the young of this species until they are 3 to 4 weeks old.

For the first few days the young snakes may naturally refuse all food until they have undergone their first moult and absorbed any remaining embryonic yolk, and some breeders routinely wait until they have sloughed a second time before offering food. If they refuse to start feeding of their own accord (this seems especially chronic in the lizard-eating West Indian C. *hortulanus*; Winstel, 1992, 1995), rearing the neonate boas can be highly problematic. Every effort should be made to persuade them to accept food voluntarily using different prey items at different times of the day. They will often feed more readily in darkness or subdued light and if the humidity is high (90–100%). If they steadfastly refuse to feed it may, as a last resort, be necessary to assist-feed them with small food items until they begin to take prey of their own accord. Probably the most convenient food source for feeding newborn tree boas in captivity is pre-killed 1- or 2-day-old mice, and these will often be accepted straight away. If mice should be refused, the neonates can be offered a variety of other small animals as a way of tempting them to start feeding. Fledgling birds such as those of quail (*Excalfactoria chinensis, Coturnix japonica* etc.), sparrows, and other small passerine birds, small frogs, and various hatchling lizards (particularly *Anolis* and *Norops* spp.) are just a few alternative food items that are known to have successfully stimulated a feeding response.

The neonates are best kept between 26 °C and 27 °C, and it is important not to keep them at too high a temperature, or accidentally let them become overheated. Temperatures above 32 °C have been known to cause inversion of the hemipenes in neonate male Emerald tree boas (Tepedelen, 1991), and should this go undetected, the snakes may lose one or both hemipenes, and possibly die. This can be treated and corrected at an early stage by soaking the snake in cool water and applying sugar directly to the hemipenes to reduce swelling.

Growth rate is primarily dependent on food intake and temperature and possibly also genetic constitution. Murphy et al. (1978) provided growth rate information for *Corallus annulatus* and *C. caninus* captive bred at the Dallas and Fort Worth Zoos; 8 neonate *C. annulatus* with a mean total length of 444 mm and mean weight of 16.4 g increased by an average of 467 mm in length and 87.6 g after 12 months; 7 neonate *C. caninus* with a mean total length of 448 mm and mean weight of 30 g increased by an average of 834 mm and 1038 g after 39 months. Gehrmann (1990) produced further data on prey mass assimilation in *C. caninus*, based on five newborn snakes (2 males and 3 females) maintained under identical and controlled environmental conditions; during the first 2 years (approximation) of life the neonates consumed a total food mass of 1335.6 g each (average) and increased by an average of 550.6 g in body mass, giving an assimilation efficiency value of 41%. Gehrmann also noted that the three females exhibited a greater period between skin sloughs than the two males, indicating a possible sexual difference.

Similarly, the time at which tree boas reach sexual maturity is dependent on much the same set of factors and possibly, to a lesser extent, age. Captive bred *C. caninus* have been observed to engage in courtship and attempt to copulate at an age of 27 months (Murphy et al., 1978), and first generation *C. hortulanus cooki* have reproduced in captivity at a size of some 0.75 meter SVL and at 25 months old (Stafford, pers. ob.).

LITERATURE CITED

Ab'Saber, A. N. 1977. Os Dominios morfoclimáticos na América do Sul: Primeira aproximação. Geomorfologia 52: 1–23.

Bartecki, U., and Heymann, E. W. 1987. Field observation of snake-mobbing in a group of Saddle-back Tamarins, *Saguinus fuscicollis nigrifrons*. Folia Primatol., 48: 199–202.

Beebe, W. 1946. Field notes on the snakes of Kartabo, British Guiana, and Caripito, Venezuela. Zoologica, 31(1): 11–52.

Blody, D. A., and Mehaffey, D. T. 1989. The reproductive biology of the Annulated boa *Corallus annulatus*. Int. Zoo Yb., 28: 167–172.

Boulenger, G. A. 1893. Catalogue of the snakes in the British Museum (Natural History), Vol. 1. Taylor and Francis, London.

Bowler, J. K. 1977. Longevity of reptiles and amphibians in North American collections as of 1st November 1975. SSAR Misc. Publs. Herpetol. Circ., No.6.

Branch, W. R. 1981. Hemipenes of the Madagascan boas *Acrantophis* and *Sanzinia*, with a review of hemipeneal morphology in the Boinae. J. Herpetol., 15: 91–99.

Brown, A. E. 1893. Notes on some snakes from tropical America lately living in the collection of the Zoological Society of Philadelphia. Proc. Acad. Nat. Sci. Philad., 8(2): 429–435.

Campbell, J. A. and Lamar, W. W. 1989. The Venomous Reptiles of Latin America. Cornell University Press, Ithaca, New York.

Chippaux, J-P. 1986. Les Serpents de la Guyane française. Fauna Tropicale XXVII. Éditions de l'Orstom, Institut français de Recherche Scientifique pour le Development en Coopération.

Cope, E. D. 1876. On the Batrachia and Reptilia of Costa Rica. J. Acad. Nat. Sci. Philad., 8(2): 93–154.

Dodd, C. K., Jr. 1986. Importation of live snakes and snake products into the United States, 1977–1983. Herpetol. Rev., 17: 76–79.

Duellman, W. E. 1978. The biology of an equatorial herpetofauna in Amazonian Equador. Misc. Publs. Mus. Nat. Hist. Univ Kans., 65: 1–352.

Dunn, E. R. 1949. Relative abundance of some Panamanian snakes. Ecology, 30: 39–57.

Felsenstein, J. 1985. Confidence limits on phylogenies: an approach using the bootstrap. Evolution, 39: 783–791.

Forcart, L. 1951. Nomenclature remarks on some generic names of the snake family Boidae. Herpetologica, 7: 197–199.

Forstner, M. R. J., Davis, S. K., Barker, D., and Barker, T. 1995. Phylogenetic analysis of the Henophidia using mitochondrial DNA sequence data. Program and Abstracts, Amer. Soc. Ichthyol. Herpetol., Amer. Elasmobr. Soc., Herpetol. League, Univ. Alberta, p. 105.

Garrett, C. M., and Smith, B. E. 1994. Perch colour preference in juvenile Green tree pythons, *Chondropython viridis*. Zoo Biology, 13: 45–50.

Gehrmann, W. H. 1990. Variation in the periodicity of defecation and ecdysis in a group of sibling Emerald tree boas, *Corallus canina*. Bull. Chicago Herpetol. Soc., 25: 67–69.

Hardy, J. D. 1957. Bat predation by the Cuban boa, *Epicrates angulifer* Bibron. Copeia, 1957: 151–152.

Hedges, S. B. 1996. The origin of West Indian amphibians and reptiles. Pp. 95–128. *In:* Powell, R., and Henderson, R. W. (Eds.), Contributions to West Indian herpetology: a tribute to Albert Schwartz. Soc. Study Amphib. Rept., Ithaca, NY. Contrib. Herpetol., Vol. 12.

Henderson, R. W. 1988. The kaleidoscopic tree boa: *Corallus enydris* in the West Indies. Lore, 38(4): 25–30.

Henderson, R. W. 1990a. Tree boas on Grenada: the colorful puzzle. Bull. Chicago Herpetol. Soc., 25(2): 21–24.

Henderson, R. W. 1990b. Correlation of environmental variables and dorsal color in *Corallus enydris* (Serpentes: Boidae) on Grenada: some preliminary results. Carib. J. Sci., 26(3–4): 166–170.

Henderson, R. W. 1993a. Foraging and diet in West Indian *Corallus enydris* (Serpentes: Boidae). J. Herpetol., 27(1): 24–28.

Henderson, R. W. 1993b. On the diets of some arboreal boids. Herpetological Natural History, 1(1): 91–96.

Henderson, R. W. 1993c. *Corallus*. Catalogue of American Amphibians and Reptiles, 572: 1–2.

Henderson, R. W. 1994. A splendid quintet: the widespread boas of South America. Lore, 44: 2–9.

Henderson, R. W., and Hedges, S. B. 1995. Origin of West Indian populations of the geographically widespread boa *Corallus enydris* inferred from mitochondrial DNA sequences. Molec. Phylogen. Evol., 4: 88–92.

Henderson, R. W., and Henderson, K. F. 1995. Altitudinal variation in body temperature in foraging tree boas (*Corallus enydris*) on Grenada. Carib. J. Sci., 31(1–2): 73–76.

Henderson, R. W., and Puorto, G. 1993. *Corallus cropanii*. Catalogue of American Amphibians and Reptiles, 575: 1–2.

Henderson, R. W., Waller, T., Miccuci, P., Puerto, G., and Bourgeois, R. W. 1995. Ecological correlates and patterns in the distribution of neotropical boines (Serpentes: Boidae): a preliminary assessment. Herpetol. Nat. Hist., 3(1): 15–27.

Henderson, R. W., and Winstel, R. A. 1992. Activity patterns, temperature relationships, and habitat utilization in *Corallus enydris* (Serpentes: Boidae) on Grenada, Carib. J. Sci., 28(3–4): 229–232.

Henderson, R. W., and Winstel, R. A. 1995. Aspects of habitat selection by an arboreal boa (*Corallus enydris*) in an area of mixed agriculture on Grenada. J. Herpetol., 29: 272–275.

Henderson, R. W., Winstel, R. A., and Friesch, J. 1996. *Corallus hortulanus* (Serpentes: Boidae) in the post-Columbian West Indies: New habitats, new prey species, and new predators. *In* Powell, R., and Henderson, R. W. (Eds.), Contributions to West Indian herpetology: A tribute to Albert Schwartz, pp. 417–423. Soc. Study Amphib. Rept., Ithaca, NY. Contrib. Herpetol., Vol. 12.

Hoge, A. R. 1953. A new genus and species of *Boinae* from Brazil. *Xenoboa cropanii*, gen. nov., sp. nov. Mem. Inst. Butantan, 25(1): 27–34.

Hopkins, H. C., and Hopkins, M. J. G. 1982. Predation by a snake of a flower-visiting bat at *Parkia nitida* (Leguminosae; Mimosoideae). Brittonia, 34(2): 225–227.

Hudson, R. 1983. The reptile reproduction program at the Fort Worth Zoo. *In:* Marcellini, D. L. (Ed.), Proceedings of 6th Annual Reptile Symposium on Captive Propagation and Husbandry: 328–349. Thurmont, MD: Zoological Consortium.

IUCN., 1979. Red Data Book 3, Amphibians and Reptiles, 3rd Ed. Compiled by R. E. Honegger. Morges, Switzerland.

Kluge, A. G. 1991. Boine snake phylogeny and research cycles. Misc. Publs. Mus. Zool. Univ. Mich., No. 178.

Kumar, S., Tamura, K., and Nei, M. 1993. MEGA, Molecular Evolutionary Genetic Analysis Software for Microcomputers. CABIOS 10: 189–191.

Laszlo, J. 1983. Further notes on reproduction patterns of amphibians and reptiles in relation to captive breeding. Int. Zoo Yb., 23: 166–174. Zoological Society of London, London.

McDiarmid, R. W., Touré, T. S., and Savage, J. M. In press. The proper name of the tropical American tree boa often referred to as *Corallus enydris* (Serpentes: Boidae). J. Herpetol.

Meyer-Holzapfel, M. 1969. Notes on the breeding and egg-laying of some reptiles at Berne Zoo. Int. Zoo Yb., 9: 20–23.

Mole, R. R., and Urich, F. W. 1894. Biological notes upon the Ophidia of Trinidad, B.W.I., with a preliminary list of the species recorded from the island. Proc. Zool. Soc. London, 1894: 499–518.

Murphy, J. B., Barker, D. G., and Tryon, B. W. 1978. Miscellaneous notes on the reproductive biology of reptiles. 2. Eleven species of the family Boidae, genera *Candoia, Corallus, Epicrates* and *Python*. J. Herpetol., 12(3): 385–390.

Niceforo-Maria, H. 1942. Los ofidios de Colombia. Rev. Acad. Ci. Exact., Fis. Nat., 5: 84–101.

Osborne, S. T. 1984. *Corallus canina* (Emerald tree boa) behaviour. Herpetol. Rev., 15(2): 50.

O'Shea, M. T. 1990. The herpetofauna of Ilha de Maracá, territory of Roraima, northern Brazil. Reptiles: Proc. 1988 U.K. Herpetol. Soc. Symp. Captive Breed., pp. 51–72.

Pérez-Santos, C., and Moreno, A. G. 1988. Ofidios de Colombia. Monografia VI, Museo Regionale di Scienze Naturali, Torino.

Peters, J. A. 1957. Taxonomic notes on Ecuadorian snakes in the American Museum of Natural History. Am. Mus. Novit., 1851(8): 1–13.

Por, F. D. 1992. Sooretama: the Atlantic Rain Forest of Brazil. SPB Academ. Publ., The Hague, Netherlands, × + 130 pp.

Puorto, G., and Henderson, R. W. 1994. Ecologically significant distribution records for the Common tree boa (Corallus enydris) in Brasil. Herpetological Natural History, 2(2): 89–91.

Rendahl, H., and Vestergren, G. 1940. Notes on Colombian Snakes. Ark. Zool., 33(1): 1–16.

Rendahl, H., and Vestergren, G. 1941. On a small collection of snakes from Ecuador. Ark. Zool., 33A(5): 1–16.

Rodríguez, G., and Reagan, D. P. 1984. Bat predation by the Puerto Rican boa (Epicrates inornatus). Copeia, 1984: 219–220.

Rzhetsky, A., and Nei, M. 1992. A simple method for estimating and testing minimum-evolution trees. Molec. Biol. Evol., 4: 406–425.

Schulte, R. 1988. Observaciones sobre la boa verde, Corallus caninus, en el Departamento San Martin—Peru. Biol. Lima, 55: 21–26.

Shaw, G. 1802. General zoology or systematic natural history. Vol. 3. Part 2. Amphibia. Thomas Davison, London.

Stafford, P.J. 1986. Notes on the distribution, habits and various colour morphs of Cook's tree boa (Corallus enydris cookii Gray). Litt. Serp., 6(4): 147–154.

Tepedelen, K. 1991. Captive propagation of the Emerald tree boa Corallus caninus. Litt. Serp., 11(6): 131–135.

Tolson, P. J., and Henderson, R. W. 1993. The natural history of West Indian boas. R & A Publ., Somerset, U.K.

Victor, M. A. M. 1975. A Devastaçao Florestal. Soc. Silvicultura, São Paulo, 48 pp.

Walls, G. L. 1942. The vertebrate eye and its adaptive radiation. Cranbrook Inst. Sci., Bull., 19.

Walsh, T. 1994. Husbandry of long-term captive populations of boid snakes (Epicrates, Corallus, and Chondropython). In: Murphy, J. B., Adler, K., and Collins, J. T. (Eds.), Captive Management and Conservation of Amphibians and Reptiles, pp. 359–362. Soc. Study Amphib. Rept., Ithaca, New York. Contrib. Herpetol., Vol. 11.

Wehekind, L. 1974. Notes on the foods of the Trinidad Snakes. Br. J. Herpetol., 2: 9–13.

Winstel, A. 1992. Observations on the care and management of Amazon and Cook's tree boas (Corallus enydris). Rept. Amphib. Mag., Sept.–Oct. 1992: 2–13.

Winstel, A. 1995. Tree boas on a tropical isle. Reptiles, 2(5): 16–22.

ADDITIONAL REFERENCE SOURCES

Anon. 1974. Zoo breeds Emerald tree boas. America's First Zoo. Philadelphia, 26(3): 30.

Abuys, A. 1981. De systematiek en kenmerken van de slangen van het genus *Corallus*. Litt. Serp., 1(6): 222–237.

Abuys, A. 1988. De tuinboa *(Corallus enydris)* in literatuur, natuur, en terrarium (1). Lacerta, 46: 194–198.

Amaral, A. 1976. Serpentes do Brazil: iconografia colorado. Univ. São Paulo, São Paulo.

Bartlett, R. D. 1986. Comments on the Amazonian tree boa *(Corallus enydris ssp.)*. Notes from NOAH, 14(2): 3–6.

Beddard, F. E. 1906. Contributions to the Knowledge of the Vascular and Respiratory Systems in the Ophidia, and to the Anatomy of the Genera *Boa* and *Corallus*. Proc. Zool. Soc. Lond., 1906: 499–532.

Beddard, F. E. 1908. A Comparison of the Neotropical Species of *Corallus, C. cookii* with *C. madagascariensis*; and on Some Points in the Anatomy of *Corallus caninus*. Proc. Zool. Soc. Lond., 1908: 135–158.

Boos, H. and Quesnel, V. 1969. Reptiles of Trinidad and Tobago. Syncolour, Port of Spain.

Dixon, J. R., and Soini, P. 1977. The reptiles of the upper Amazon basin, Iquitos region, Peru. Part 2. crocodilians, turtles and snakes. Contribs. Biol. Geol. Milwaukee Pub. Mus., 12: 1–91.

Duellman, W. E. 1989. Tropical herpetofaunal communities: patterns of community structure in neotropical rainforests. *In:* Harmelin-Vivien, M. L., and Bourliere, F. (Eds.), Vertebrates in complex tropical systems. Ecol. Stud., 69, pp. 61–68. Springer-Verlag, New York.

Duellman, W. R. 1990. Herpetofaunas in neotropical rainforests: comparative composition, history, and resource use. *In:* Gentry, A. H. (Ed.), Four neotropical rainforests, pp. 455–505. Yale University Press, New Haven.

Dunn, J. 1993. Grenada's serene serpents: the real story behind the tree boa. Save the Earth J., 2: 8.

Eerden, H. van der. 1986. Striking behaviour of *Corallus enydris enydris* in the terrarium. Litt. Serp., 6(4): 126.

Eerden, H. van der. 1987. The breeding of *Corallus enydris enydris* in a terrarium. Litt. Serp., 7(5): 243–246.

Emsley, M. G. 1977. Snakes, Trinidad and Tobago. Bull. Maryland Herpetol. Soc., 13: 210–304.

Foekema, G. M. M. 1974. Enkele notities over *Corallus enydris* (slanke boomboa), met een verslag over verzorging en gedrag van drie *Corallus enydris cookii* in een uiskamerterrarium. Lacerta, 32(9–10): 151–164.

Gaige, H. T., Hartweg, N., and Stuart, L. C. 1937. Notes on a collection of amphibians and reptiles from eastern Nicaragua. Occ. Pap. Mus. Zool., Univ. Michigan, 357: 1–18.

Gobels, M. 1985. Haltung und Nachzucht des Hundkopfschlingers *Corallus caninus* Linnaeus, 1758 im Terrarium. Salamandra, 21: 137–147.

Golder, F. 1985. Haltung und Zucht sowie Umfärbung der Jungschlangen von *Corallus caninus* (Linnaeus, 1758). Salamandra, 21: 148–156.

Greene, H. W. 1988. Antipredator mechanisms in reptiles. *In:* Gans, C., and Huey, R. B. (Eds.), Biology of the Reptilia, Vol. 16, Ecology, Defence and Life History. Alan R. Liss, Inc., New York.

Groves, J. D. 1978. Observations on the reproduction of the Emerald tree boa, *Corallus caninus*. Herpetol. Review, 9(3): 100–102.

Güney, O. 1993. Captive breeding of the Emerald tree boa. Annual Journal of the Association for the Study of Reptilia and Amphibia, pp. 60–67.

Güney, O. 1995. Captive breeding of the Emerald tree boa. Vivarium, 7(3): 18–23.

Henderson, R. W. 1991. Distribution and preliminary interpretation of geographic variation in the neotropical tree boa *Corallus enydris*: a progress report. Bull. Chicago Herpetol. Soc., 26(5): 105–110.

Henderson, R. W. 1992. Significant distribution records for some amphibians and reptiles in the Lesser Antilles. Carib. J. Sci., 28(1–2): 101–103.

Henderson, R. W. 1993d. *Corallus annulatus*. Catalogue of American Amphibians and Reptiles, 573: 1–3.

Henderson, R. W. 1993e. *Corallus caninus*. Catalogue of American Amphibians and Reptiles, 574: 1–4.

Henderson, R. W. 1993f. *Corallus enydris*. Catalogue of American Amphibians and Reptiles, 576: 1–6.

Henderson, R. W., and Boos, H. E. A. 1993. The tree boa (*Corallus enydris*) on Trinidad and Tobago. Living World, J. Trinidad & Tobago Field Natur. Club, 1994–1994: 3–5.

Huff, T. A. 1980. Captive propagation of the subfamily Boinae with emphasis on the genus *Epicrates*. *In:* Reproductive Biology and Diseases of Captive Reptiles. SSAR Contribs. Herpetol., 1: 125–134.

Kreutz, R. 1989. "Ballstellung" bei der Gartenboa *Corallus enydris* (Linnaeus, 1758). Salamandra, 25: 115–116.

Lillywhite, H. B., and Henderson, R. W. 1993. Behavioral and functional ecology of arboreal snakes. *In:* Siegel, R. A., and Collins, J. T. (Eds.), Snakes: Ecology and Behaviour, pp. 1–48. McGraw-Hill, New York.

Mole, R. R. 1924. The Trinidad snakes. Proc. Zool. Soc. London, 1924: 235–278.

Oxtoby, G. P. 1989. Zwangerschap van een uitzonderlijk jonge Cooks tuinboa (*Corallus enydris cookii*). Lacerta, 47: 112–116.

Pendelbury, G. B. 1974. Stomach and intestine contents of *Corallus enydris*: a comparison of island and mainland forms. J. Herpetol., 8: 241–244.

Pérez-Santos, C., and Moreno, A. G. 1991. Serpientes de Ecuador. Monografia XI, Museo Regionale di Scienze Naturali, Torino.

Peters, J. A., and Orejas-Miranda, B. 1970. Catalogue of the neotropical squamata. Part 1, Snakes. Bull. U.S. Natl. Mus., 297(1): 1–347.

Peters, U. 1961. *Corallus annulatus*. D.A.T.Z., 14: 62.

Pols, J. J. van der. 1981. Care and breeding of *Corallus enydris enydris*. Litt. Serp., 1(6): 238–245.

Rand, A. S., and Myers, C. W. 1990. The herpetofauna of Barro Col-
ourado Island, Panama: an ecological summary. *In:* Gentry, A. H.
(Ed.), Four neotropical rainforests, pp. 386–409. Yale University
Press, New Haven.

Reil, C. A. P. van. 1984. Reproduction of *Corallus caninus* Linnaeus,
1758 in captivity. Litt. Serp., 4(5–6): 173–181.

Rodríguez, L. B., and Cadle, J. E. 1990. A preliminary overview of the
herpetofauna of Cocha Cashu, Manu National Park, Peru. *In:*
Gentry, A. H. (Ed.), Four neotropical rainforests, pp. 410–425.
Yale University Press, New Haven.

Ross, R. A., and Marzec, G. 1990. The Reproductive Husbandry of
Pythons and Boas. Instit. Herpetol. Res., Stamford, California.

Schwartz, A., and Henderson, R. W. 1991. Amphibians and Reptiles
of the West Indies: descriptions, distributions, and natural history. Univ. Florida Press, Gainesville.

Sexton, O. J., and Heatwole, H. F. 1965. Life-history notes on some
Panamanian snakes. Carib. J. Sci., 5: 39–43.

Stafford, P. J. 1981. Observations on the captive breeding of Cook's
tree boa *(Corallus enydris cookii)*. The Herptile, 6(4): 15–17.

Stemmler, O., and Vesely, Z. 1968. Eine interesante Form der Gartenboa *(Corallus enydris ssp.* non det*)* von Venezuela. Aqua. Terra., 5:
38–39.

Wagner, E. 1985. Captive husbandry of wild-caught Emerald tree
boas. *In:* Gray, R. L. (Ed.), Proc. North. California Herpetol. Soc.
and Bay Area Amphib. Rept. Soc. Conf. on Captive Propagation
and Husbandry of Reptiles and Amphibians. pp. 109–111.

Walsh, T. 1978. Husbandry and breeding of *Corallus caninus* at the
National Zoological Park, with notes on thermoregulation of
gravid females. Unpubl. Man., 21 pp.

Willard, D. E. 1977. Constricting methods of snakes. Copeia, 1977:
379–382.

Winstel, A. 1987. Breeding the Amazon tree boa *(Corallus enydris
enydris)*. Litt. Serp., 7(6): 267–271.

Winstel, A. 1988. The Amazon tree boa's amazing colours. Vivarium,
1(3): 5–7.

Winstel, A. 1989. Herpetoculture of the Amazon tree boa. Vivarium,
1(4): 12–14.

Winstel, A. 1990. Husbandry and display potential of the Amazon
tree boa *(Corallus enydris enydris)*. Anim. Keepers Forum, 17: 386–
387.

Zimmerman, B. L., and Rodrigues, M. T. 1990. Frogs, snakes, and lizards of the INPA-WWF reserves near Manaus, Brazil. *In:* Gentry, A. H. (Ed.), Four neotropical rainforests, pp. 426–454. Yale University Press, New Haven.

INDEX

Page numbers in boldface type indicate location of relevant figures. Color plate numbers are also referenced.

84